Bedtime Stories
For Adults:

Restore your Body and Mind with Relaxing
Short Stories designed to prevent Insomnia,
Reduce Anxiety and Enhance Deep Sleep.
Stress Relief and Self Healing Hypnosis

Claire Watts

Table of Contents

Introduction

Sleep is something that everyone should consider more than normal. Adults and children walk around town less tired than ever before and in order to make things worse, their days are far more busy than in years and it is important that there are ample rest to perform the tasks of the next day every day.

When you continue to get sick, feel very sleepy, or even if for no reason you find that you gain weight, it may be time for more sleep. When your body sleeps without the energy required, your body will have to do all the work, play and school can become a constant fight.

Society becomes increasingly vulnerable to being ill, overweight, and many are dependent on drugs to get them through the day, and to cure illnesses that would otherwise not happen, if each adult had enough time to sleep almost a hundred years ago, an average of 9-10 hours a day.

Most adults today at best have an average of six or seven. When you lose sleep, your body automatically starts looking for additional calories to make up for sleep and give your body sufficient energy to get through the day. Lack of sleep also regulates the body's quantity of fat and how your appetite functions.

Most adults too are consumed by the digital wave of interaction, which keeps them on the loop by watching TV, surfing the Internet, listening to music and all the other products everybody has these days abused.

Rather than watching TV before bed, reading is a great way to get better. It's also more enjoyable and has a way to relax and sleep more naturally. Eating high-carbon foods such as pastas is a simple way to lose sleep.

You need too much time to eat the sort of heavy food at night, and in the middle of the night you wake up to try to process it all. Only step a few hours before bedtime away from heavy foods and drink a glass of milk or green tea to relax.

Your sleep pattern will have full control over your eating schedule, so if you want to lose weight, it is important that you have enough rest. No lunch, try to choose protein every morning and any fruit you can even sprout during your morning travel will be enough.

At least nine hours a night, trying to sleep may seem like an impossible task. Make it a priority to shut down mobile phones, laptops and TVs. Even if you have to change your routine, you can sleep in the morning, then wake up at nine and show up at six.

In the East you will have additional daylight to do things; when you stay late, you will not be able to complete as many tasks as you can when you get up earlier.

Health sleep disorders are becoming more prevalent. The use of drugs can cause side effects that lead to poor sleep. And older people suffer from more sleeping medical and mental conditions.

The good news is that all of these sleep problems can be handled effectively. Good sleep at any age is possible. The key is to understand the changes in our sleep as we grow old and then get to the root cause of problems.

There are several shifts to normal sleep as we get older. Deep sleep and sleep diminish slowly as we pass from late adulthood into old age. We wake up more often during the night, even more often than the average 12 to 15 cycles during young adulthood.

Therefore, our sleep is less productive because we are awake for a large percentage of our time in bed. We often start taking naps to make up for less efficient sleep. Most senior citizens settle in a routine of two naps every day over time. One in the middle of the morning and one in the middle of the day.

The sleep pattern for infants and young children is identical. Yet elderly people don't come fully "full cycle" and stick to childhood sleep patterns. There are much more distinctions than similarities.

In a 24-hour cycle, for instance, the elderly do not need much sleep, as children do. Indeed, when we get older, the amount of sleep we need, although there is some discussion on this point.

But we needed a little less sleep for many years as we grew older. Generally speaking, people sleep about 30 minutes lower than young adults as seniors. Yet new thinking questions if less sleep necessarily means less sleep for the elderly. Studies have shown that people sleep more easily during old age than young adults during the day.

Combined stress over numerous years has likewise been involved in the improvement of nervousness conditions, and a distressing way of life that keeps away from work out, solid nourishment, day by day unwinding, social help, and self-sustaining exercises can put you at expanded hazard. Long periods of substantial smoking regularly go before nervousness disorders, particularly agoraphobia, summed up uneasiness, and frenzy disorder. The affiliation radiates an impression of being debilitated by a breathing limit. Your serotonin level might be included, particularly on the off chance that you create over the top habitual characteristics

Chapter 1. College Sweethearts

When Carole and Jordon were freshmen in college, they met at a coffee cart outside of the main entrance to the old campus lot. Their meeting was like one straight out of a storybook, complete with cool fall weather, colorful leaves strewn about, and cozy scarves, and toques adorning everyone to help them stay warm. One morning in the fall of freshman year, Carole was standing with her friends in line at the coffee cart and Jordon was working the cart to earn some extra cash to help purchase new filming equipment. When Carole was next in line, she walked up to the cart and ordered an Americano with extra whip cream. "Odd order," Jordon answered, scribbling it down on a piece of paper. "Whip cream on coffee?" He asked. "Just the way I like it." Carole smiled, handing Jordon exact change for her drink. As she handed him the change, Carole and Jordon locked eyes and smiled, pausing for a moment to take in the simple and sweet beauty of falling in love with each other.

Carole thought Jordon was attractive, so she made a mental note of which cart he was working at and came back to that cart each morning for weeks after. Some mornings, Jordon would be working and he would prepare her drink for her. Others, he would not be working but he would always seem to be nearby the cart so that when she was done ordering they could share some conversation before they each parted ways to attend their respective classes. Without ever telling the other, the two of them always did their best to ensure that they would see each other every single morning.

Carole and Jordon grew fond of their morning conversations. They also started getting braver and braver as they each began leaving little hints about having an attraction toward the other. Carole would always smile and give Jordon a hug if he was not working, and Jordon would always draw little smiley faces or hearts on Carole's Americano with the whipped cream. These two lovers had a great deal of fun falling for each other and enjoy casually flirting with one another each morning before classes.

One day, during the middle of winter, when it was particularly cold outside, Jordon proposed that the two of them head inside and grab a bite to eat. It just so happened that Carole did not have to be at class for another forty-five minutes, so she agreed and the two of them walked together to the cafeteria hall to eat their breakfasts with each other. They spent the entire time laughing, enjoying each other's company, and falling even more deeply in love with each other.

When the breakfast was done, the two parted ways and went to their respective classes. All morning, they both found themselves distracted by thoughts of the other. They loved how it felt so normal to be with each other, and how spending time together seemed to come so easily. When their classes were over that day, Carole went back to her dorm to study. At some point that evening, she heard a knock at her door. When she answered it, she saw none other than Jordon standing there, smiling, with his hands stuffed in his pockets. He paused for a moment before asking if she wanted to go to the library with him to study together, and Carole happily agreed. The two of them spent the evening studying, joking, and enjoying each other's company.

After that, Carole and Jordon began hanging out almost daily. They would share breakfast, study sessions, or even just walks around the campus as they enjoyed each other's presence. When spring break came, they carpooled back to see their family as they both came from the same small town in Connecticut. They would listen to their favorite songs on the ride back home, sing, laugh, and spend even more time getting to know each other along the way.

As the years went by, Carole and Jordon became inseparable. In sophomore year, they spent spring break on a vacation together in Cape Cod where they enjoyed delicious seafood dinners and beach walks together each evening. In junior year, they spent Christmas at each other's family's houses, enjoying two dinners, and sharing the opportunity to meet each other's extended families. By senior year, they fell so deeply in love that there was no way these two could be separated from each other's company.

When graduation was right around the corner, Jordon began acting strange. Carole thought he was reconsidering their relationship since college would be over soon and became worried that the love of her life was preparing to leave her. Jordon became scared because he had no idea what the love of his life would think about him wanting to spend the rest of their lives together. Shortly after the two walked across the stage, Jordon got down on one knee and proposed to Carole. He proposed that she marry him, that they move in together, that they start their careers, and that they eventually have the children and dogs that they always dreamed about having during their late night study sessions. Carole cried as she realized that Jordon had been acting weird because he was about to propose, not because he was preparing to leave her. She said yes, and the two cried together as they celebrated the reality that they would go on to live the rest of their lives together. The two lived happily ever after, as they say in the fairy tales.

Chapter 2. Bergen

As I lay in my bed, I can tell that it has snowed overnight. Even before I open my eyes, my ears tell me there is a blanket of effortlessly soft snow covering my world. Encouraging it to wake as slowly and quietly as I am. I lay still for a moment and recall my dream. I am flying over the turquoise Fjords of Norway's coastline, skimming along the top of the water, occasionally dipping my fingers into the sea and forming a wake which creates an operatic effect behind me. I wrestle with the idea of staying in bed under the mountain of cozy blankets, lost in a pile of pillows, trying to get back to the magical moment of flight. Still, the idea of enjoying the peaceful sights of the season's first snowfall is magnetic. It pulls my legs out from under the covers. My feet reach the ground and signal me to rise. I stretch my arms up as far as they will go and take in a deep breath, listening for the gentle footsteps of any wildlife wandering outside my window. All I hear is the quiet hum of the furnace whir to life, so I stand and reach for my robe. It's a substantial robe, more like a blanket with sleeves and a belt. Holes are forming in the elbows from season after season of transitioning me into life's activities that keep me from the warm embrace of bed for entirely too long each day.

In the kitchen, I put on the kettle at the window; I pull open the curtains and notice a sparkle of streetlights on fresh snow, creating a subtle glow across surfaces in the light's path. The sky isn't done yet and is still depositing tiny layers of winter charm across the city. Snow hugs every surface; each branch individually buried by a miniature snowbank; the mailbox is doubled in height by the season's offerings. While I wait for the kettle, I look over the undisturbed landscape of our street, and to no surprise, there isn't a single step that has broken the spell. The whole neighborhood is a sea of tiny diamonds glistening in the pre-sunrise glow, putting on its show for an audience of one. The kettle whistles, I steep my tea and prepare a small bag of snacks for my upcoming winter adventure.

I trade my blanket-robe for strategic layers of winter clothing, finishing my outfit with my favorite toque. It is topped by an enormous pompom that serves no purpose other than my amusement. I planned for this day and left my snowshoes by the front door waiting for their big moment. With my snacks and tea in my backpack, I take my first step into the uninterrupted blanket of snow awaiting me. It gives way under my boot with the satisfying, muffled crunch of snowflakes compacting under the weight of an eager winter admirer. I make my way from the front door to the main sidewalk, enjoying every individual step. I swing open the gate, and it creates a sweeping pattern in the snow, like one half of a snow angel. I strap myself into my snowshoes and begin to gingerly float atop the snow and make my way down the mountain to the picturesque neighborhood of Bryggen that line the harbor.

The roads in Bergen are a series of switchbacks up and down mountainsides, and nearly every home has a front-row view of the spectacular Fjords of the North Sea. They have been a protective maze of rock and water shielding Norwegians from those too faint of heart to navigate amongst the glacial beasts rising up from the depth of the sea. Winding my way slowly through the vacant, narrow streets, I admire frost crystallized on branches that hang heavy with the weight of an early snow. Some still have leaves on them, red and yellow poke out from the clean white cover as the soft orange and pink of the rising sun creates an iridescent light show across the snowy boughs. Daylight slowly climbs into the sky and washes over the city.

The perfectly symmetrical peaks of the heritage buildings of Bryggen appear as I reach the bottom of the hill. More neighbors have joined me in my early morning appreciation of the season's finest offerings. The commercial buildings, once home to warehouses for the trading activity of the region, are now lit up and decorated with modern housewares, jewelers, and galleries. A few pubs dot the main road, and the patios which typically seat hundreds of tourists are empty patches of undisturbed poufs of snow. I meander my way across the open landscape, creating a circular pattern to be found by the cafe staff when they open and shovel out the patio for the day's visitors.

At the end of the harbor, a tall ship has docked, sails drawn in to be protected from the elements. The masts rise proudly into the now clear sky of this early winter morning. I picture its hull filled with spices from far off lands, silk tapestries embroidered by someone on the other side of the globe, and a treasure so rare the ship captain is unaware of its worth. Still, I know what they have stowed on that boat and am here to relieve them of it. I use my mitted hand to sweep snow off a bench and take a seat. The tea in my backpack releases a plume of steam into the air as I open it and wrap my hands around the thermos. Taking in its warmth and fragrant aroma of apple and cinnamon spice. In the shadow of this great ship, on the doorstep of history, I pause and wonder how many winter adventurers sat in this same spot. Staring into the mystery of the sea, preparing themselves for the next leg of their journey across this spectacular land. I take the snacks out from my backpack and secretly hope someone comes by willing to make a trade.

Chapter 3. The Arrangement

Since their childhood, it was known, accepted, and understood that Lidia would marry Ander. This arrangement had been made before either of them were able to speak. This arrangement kept Lidia and Ander close and children. Growing up, they had become best friends and spent all their time laughing, singing, and playing together.

Getting to marry your best friend, the children always thought, would be such a great way to do things. You wouldn't have to worry whether your husband was going to be boring or stinky. You wouldn't have to worry if your wife didn't like the same things as you or that she was a really bad singer. The children had decided that they were happy to grow up to marry one another.

The wedding date had been set for a spring wedding after Lidia had turned 18 when Ander would be 19. They had settled on an outdoor ceremony that would take place near the pond in their village. Lidia had chosen the flowers she wanted for the ceremony and every detail had been beautifully planned.

Lidia sat in her father's shop one morning, working on finalizing some of the finer points of the wedding when a customer walked through the door. He was tall and raven-haired with the most striking green eyes Lidia had ever seen. He smiled at Lidia and asked her something she didn't hear over the beating of her heart when she saw him.

"What? Oh, I'm sorry, I didn't hear you. What did you say?" Lidia closed her eyes for a moment and shook her head. He chuckled.

"I said, 'Does this shop take special commissions?' I wish to build a wooden chest, but I haven't the skill to do it myself."

"Yes, we do take commissions for custom wooden pieces. May I ask what you'll be using the chest for and if you have any specifics in mind?"

"I wish to use the chest to store clothing from the winter. I don't need it in the hotter months and wish to keep them safe from any moths or pests that would eat away at them. I'm not particularly picky about the style that is used to make it, but I was thinking that walnut wood would be ideal." Lidia took down all the relevant notes for the project so her father would be able to get started on the project for him.

"May I have your name?"

"I'm Aleksei. I live just on the far end of town. When should I come back to pick up the piece?"

"Two weeks is the current estimate. If that changes, we'll send a letter to let you know when you can come pick it up, unless you would like it delivered to your house."

"No, I can come pick it up; that will be fine." Lidia's heart raced as she completed the transaction with Aleksei. She was completely smitten with the slight upturn at the end of his nose and the olive glow his skin seemed to have.

"Are you new to the villáge? I haven't seen you around before." Lidia felt as though the words had found their own way out of her mouth before she could stop them.

"Yes, I am!" Aleksei seemed delighted to know he had moved to a place in which those from other places were noticed. "I just moved to the edge of the village in the last fortnight. I have decided the climate here is much more ideal and the people are very friendly. I just wish I knew more people and of more places to go."

"Well, if you would like someone to help you familiarize yourself with the town, I'd love to help you." He smiled at her coyly.

"Thank you for the offer; perhaps I will." He took the receipt Lidia had written for him and slipped it into his pocket before turning around to leave the shop. Just as he did, it was as though someone had let all the air out of Lidia, causing her to deflate.

Aleksei was gorgeous and there was nothing that he couldn't ask of her at this point. She felt her heart leap when she spoke to him and she felt like she could never let go of the image of his face. As she completed her workday, the image of his smile would drift through her head from time to time. In spite of herself and her duties, she would find herself feeling giddy each time it happened.

When she went home and her mother asked her questions about the wedding, which was only a couple of weeks away, she hardly took notice. She had looked out the window and saw Ander walking down the road. She hopped up out of her seat, hardly taking notice of the fact that she was blowing off her mother by walking out of the house and talking to Ander.

"There's someone new in town," she mentioned as she sidled up to him on his walk down the road.

"I heard about that. Turns out he is from across the sea and has decided to live here permanently instead. I wonder why he left his home."

"Maybe it was boring, and the people were stuffy," Lidia posited.

"Well, then he moved to the wrong place to fix it." Lidia laughed at Ander's snipe.

"Maybe we should try to make friends with him. We have so few friends our age and it would be so nice if we had more than just our parents for company, don't you think?" Ander looked at her and smiled.

"You're so sweet. You're right; we could use more friends our age. My mother taught me how to play mahjongg yesterday so she and her friends could have a fourth player on weeks when Doris is visiting her son." Ander gazed off into the distance.

They arranged to meet with Aleksei at a tavern in the middle of town that evening to get to know him.

When they got to the table, they ordered drinks and began talking and getting to know one another. Before long, Aleksei and Lidia were finishing one another's sentences. The world fell away and they both talked at length about their lives, their interests, and their experiences.

"Lidia," Ander piped up after quite some time. He nearly startled Lidia in simply speaking, as she had all but forgotten he was there. "Can I speak to you privately for a moment?" Aleksei looked a little nervous and slightly ashamed at the question, but Lidia agreed and followed Ander through the front door of the tavern.

Once they were out of earshot, Ander took Lidia's hands. "Are you okay, honey?" Lidia looked down at her hands in Ander's and then looked at her betrothed.

"Why do you ask?"

"I ask because I have never seen you light up like that before. The way you were talking to Aleksei... I see love in your eyes." Her cheeks reddened, her heart rate increased, and her breathing became shallow. She looked back at Ander, who had sadness and concern in his eyes.

"I've never felt like this before, Ander. I have no idea what is happening to me." She looked desperate. Ander hung his head at these words, then looked at Lidia and nodded with tears in his eyes.

"It's love, baby. You're in love… For the first time." He breathed deeply as he said those words, realizing that they weren't about him. Lidia understood and looked at Ander with a pleading look. "I think we should call off the wedding. You can't marry someone that you don't love. Especially when there is someone that you do love right in front of you."

"Ander, I can't do this to you. We're betrothed and we're best friends. We've always said how wonderful it would be to marry one another. We can do this."

"No, Lid. You need to marry for love. I know how passionate you are, and I have seen the way your heart sings when you are truly invested in something wonderful. I also… don't want to settle for someone who doesn't love me." He wiped the tears from his eyes, and he looked at Lidia. "It's better for us to realize that this isn't true love before the wedding."

With heavy hearts about the plans they had been making since their childhood, Ander and Lidia approached their parents together. They cried and admitted that what they shared was little more than a friendship that would last a lifetime. Lidia's father softened at the sight of her tears and pleading gaze. The heads of the families relented and dissolved the agreement to marry their families and simply combined business ventures instead.

Lidia and Ander committed to running the business when their fathers retired, keeping their customers happy and keeping the town supplied with quality workmanship and goods.

Some months after the betrothal had been dissolved, Lidia and Aleksei were given her parents' blessing to begin a courtship.

Chapter 4. Something Is Different

Hannah wakes up one morning and something is funny. Something feels different than usual. But what is it? Hannah looks around. Everything is in its place. The night light is on the bedside table and Bruno is sitting on the floor next to the bed.

Bruno is Hannah's favorite stuffed animal. A little white dog with a straw hat and dungarees. For a long time, Bruno slept in bed. But Hannah is growing and so is not as much space in bed as before. In addition, Hannah is firmly convinced that Bruno has told her that he prefers to take care of her at night instead of sleeping. And that's a good thing - think Hannah!

Hannah slips off the bed, barefoot on the carpet. The carpet also feels as it always has. Funny! But no matter, Hannah thinks. She grabs Bruno under the arm and runs to mom and dad in the bedroom.

With a proper jump she jumps into the parents' bed and shouts, "Get up! I'm awake!". Hannah's mom and dad are still very sleepy. "Are you hungry honey?" Mum asks. Hannah thinks. "Hm, I think I could eat pancakes." Mum laughs: "We cannot quite do it my darling. Today is kindergarten again. But tomorrow is the weekend. I'd like to make some pancakes for you. "

Hannah snaps her arms up: "Yes, weekend and pancakes." Then she jumps off the bed. "Come on Mom. We make breakfast fast and then kindergarten. Then it's really weekend! "

On the way to the kitchen Hannah tells her mom what happened today - that anything feels weird. Mom touches Hannah's forehead. "Hm. So - you do not have a fever. Take A. "Hannah opens her mouth wide and sticks out her tongue:" Ahhhhhhh. "But Mom shakes her head. "Everything's fine, too," she says.

As Hannah bites into the breakfast sandwich, she is startled. "Ow!" She calls. "What's up?" Mum asks. Hannah touches her finger in her mouth. "Hoa." She says with her finger in her mouth. Then she pulls out her finger. "There's a tooth wobbling!" She says indignantly.

Mama smiles: "Oh, you have a wiggle tooth. That explains a lot. Show me. "But Hannah quickly closes her mouth and shakes her head. Then she says, "No! I do not want to go to the dentist. "Mama strokes her cheek."Darling, you do not have to go to the dentist with a wiggle."

Hannah makes big eyes. "Not?" She asks. "No!" Says Mom. "A jiggle falls out by itself. And when the time comes, we put it under your pillow at night. "" Ieeeee!"Interrupts Hannah's mom. "I'm not putting my tooth under my pillow."

Again, the mother smiles and says: "But only then can the tooth fairy get him. The next morning the tooth is gone and there is a coin there. "Hannah looks at Mum in disbelief. "Why is that?" She asks. "Because the tooth fairy does it," Mama answers.

Hannah does not quite understand that. "A fairy fetches my tooth and gives me money for it?" That makes Hannah think. "How much do I get for a tooth?" And immediately her finger disappears in her mouth again. "Uond waviel teeth hoeh ich then?"

"Enough to get rich," Mom jokes. But Hannah does not take that as a joke. "I knew it!" She calls and rubs her hands.

At kindergarten, Hannah eagerly talks about the Tooth Fairy. Jonas says tiredly: "Oh, about Zahnfee. This is definitely a mouse that steals the tooth. "But what does Jonas know? Jonas is stupid, thinks Hannah.

"Not at all!" Sandra intervened suddenly. "I've already put a tooth under my pillow and the next day there was money and the tooth was gone. So! "Then Jonas sticks out her tongue:" Bäääääh! "

Nevertheless, Hannah's sentence does not go out of her mind all day long. When Daddy picks up Hannah, she folds her arms and says, "I do not want a mouse to go under my pillow." Daddy looks at Hannah in amazement. "What mouse?" He asks. "Well, the tooth mouse." Hannah answers precociously. "Jonas says there is no tooth fairy. If I put my wiggle tooth under my pillow, then a mouse comes and fetches it. "

"Oh, Hannah," Dad says. "There is no tooth mouse! Do not listen to everything that's being told. "Hannah's stomach growls as loud as a bear. "Haven't you eaten anything?" Dad asks in astonishment. Hannah turns away: "When I eat, my tooth falls out and then the mouse comes!"

Hannah's dad squats down and nudges Hannah. "The only mouse here is you," he whispers. "If your tooth is under the pillow, there comes a beautiful tiny little fairy. She is very happy about your tooth. And because you no longer need him, she buys him from you. That's all."

Hannah turns to her daddy: "And you are quite sure?" Hannah's father smiles and nudges her again: "Absolutely!" He says in a firm voice. "Alright! Then I want a huge dinner now. "Says Hannah and pulls her arms apart.

A few days later, it is actually time. Hannah's Wackelzahn finally falls out while eating. Hannah is really excited. She was never as fast at bed-making as she is today. When Mama says good night and begins to read a story, Hannah is fidgeting all the time. "What's going on?" Asks Hannah's mom. "I do not know exactly where to put my tooth down," she says restlessly, holding up her wobble tooth.

Hannah's mom takes the tooth and puts it under the pillow. "Well my sweetheart. Here he is exactly right. But now listen to the story and then sleep well. Because the fairy only comes when you sleep. "Hannah nods and listens to the story." I cannot sleep tonight," she thinks. But before she knows it, she has already fallen asleep.

The next morning, she wakes up and slides barefoot on the floor. When she feels the carpet, she suddenly remembers the wobbly tooth. She quickly reaches for the pillow to check. The tooth is actually gone. She pulls the pillow off the bed and at the same moment she hears something falling on the carpet - a coin. She looks at the coin in amazement and whispers: "The tooth fairy was there." Then she grabs the money and runs happily to her parents. Again and again she calls, "They exist. Look, they really exist! "She runs straight into her daddy's arms. "Ui, with so much energy." Dad says as he takes Hannah up. Mom is making breakfast. "I said that," she laughs.

Hannah struggles with her legs. This is the sign for dad to let her down again. Once at the bottom, she stands straight up and holds the coin up. "I will show Jonas. He'll look around, "she says cheekily and everyone laughs heartily.

Then Hannah thinks for a moment and says: "Do you know what? I will always put all my wobbly teeth under my pillow. And when I'm rich, we all go for ice cream! "Mom and Dad think the idea is great, and Hannah is proud to have lost her first shaky tooth - or rather, to have sold!

Chapter 5.Cave of Benagil

There is a place in Portugal called the Cave of Benagil. I knew nothing about it, but my twin sister Leah had really hammered it into my head that we would be going there on our birthday. We lived in different cities, but we always made an effort to be together on holidays. Our birthday was one occasion that we were not so quick to hand over to our large family, and we often took trips to exotic places when the day came around. We were both turning thirty-five this year, and if I am honest, I was scared. Life seemed to be speeding by me at a pace that I could not fathom. I had expressed this to my twin who seemed to empathize but also told me not to worry. She told me not to research the cave at all, and I kept that promise.

The boat ride was a quick and thrilling ride alongside the rough and rocky edges of the mountainous shore. I watched as the outline of land changed before my eyes. The sky was a beautiful and inviting blue on that day, painted with thin wisps of white clouds. I looked to my side to see my sister with her eyes closed and a huge smile plastered across her tan cheeks. People had always commented on our smile being endearing; I had always brushed those words off until this moment. Her caramel-colored hair was whipping around her face as the boat seemed to jump and skid across the surface of the water.

I began to notice that these changing and jagged shorelines were quite aerated. They looked like the fizz at the top of a soda. Upon closer inspection, they were filled with caves. I had never seen anything like this place before, but it made sense that we were venturing into cave territory. At that moment, I realized that I had never even so much as contemplated a cave before. What is it like inside of one of those holes? Is it damp and cold like the movies?

Before I was even aware of what was happening, we came across a huge opening in the rock. I say huge, but a larger vessel than our little tour boat would have been hard-pressed to fit through the entrance. It was such a unique sight to behold, the way the sedimentary rock seemed to shift around a void of darkness. The light of the sun was preventing me from making out anything other than a drastic change in contrast. As we ventured into the threshold, we entered a hallway-like area, and at the end of that was an even smaller cutout.

At this point, I was beginning to get nervous. My sister must have noticed because she put a comforting hand upon my shoulder as though she were telling me to control my fear until we were on the other side. I believe that this whole trip was a testament to the trust that we had between us, as I was venturing into everything with no knowledge of the actual place. We could be going for a dangerous round of cave-diving for all I knew. The whole boat seemed to gasp as we passed through the tiny opening. Those guides must have their precision really down.

The cave was just a small tunnel that u-turned back into the ocean. I believe that the point of that particular cave was to give all of us tourists a fright. It worked though; my blood was really pumping for a moment before I relaxed again in the light of the sun. There were many more small caves, such as this one. We were in and out of them in our tiny tour boat, everyone becoming more and more excited as we went on. I was so blown away by seeing the inside of the caves that I will admit that I thought that this was the whole point of the trip. I thought that boating through narrow caves was supposed to be the fun part and I was having a great time after I got the hang of it and really learned to trust our guides.

Some of the larger caves seemed to capture just enough sunlight to cause a reflection of the water on the roof of the cavern. I watched the stone as the ripples changed direction. Caves have such a unique scent to them also. I suppose it is the smell of wet rock and sea air, but my lungs were happily consuming the wonders around me. Slowly the caves were growing in expanse, and some of them even had holes at the top that also let golden light flood through them.

I was so pleased with the trip. As we approached our next entrance, my sister turned to me and told me that this is what she wanted me to see. A cathedral that nature made within the shore. She told me that long ago she had decided to let go of the stresses of our culture. Everything human is a social construct, including our age and even time itself. None of that was real, and it wasn't worth being so wound up in. This was real. The ocean, the rocks, and the tide were real. I just gazed at her in disbelief. First of all, jump off your high horse. I will confess that I did eventually come around to her way of thinking.

We entered this cave to see a giant hole in the top. The waves lapped at a sandy shore where you could get out and really behold this natural marvel. The beauty of this particular cave brought a tear to my eye. At that moment, all of my worries did seem to melt away. The grand size and marbling in the rock, the open ceiling and the profundity of it all took me by surprise. We stayed in this cave for a moment before venturing to another that was very similar, passing arches of sediment on the way. I found myself feeling like a child again that day. I was absorbed by the tide and the majesty of Mother Nature.

Chapter 6. Meal Plan for Mice

The biggest family of all the mice families in town was the Squeakerton family. Milton was the youngest son of the family. The biggest family in town was still not so different from other families of mice, however. For one thing, mice are known to live in big families in general, so even though the Squeakertons had a bigger family than most, they were still pretty much like everyone else. Milton had ten siblings, a mom and a dad, and two grandparents who lived with them.

The house was pretty crowded, just like you would expect for such a big family. But Milton still got his own room, because they still had plenty of rooms left to spare.

Milton really liked having his own room, because he could do whatever he wanted without having to deal with his other siblings. He was the kind of mouse who liked to spend a lot of time alone reading, and being around his siblings could make it hard to focus on something like reading a book. Their house was underneath the basement of a library. That meant Milton got to read as many books as he wanted, at least as long as his family didn't want him to do something else.

If they wanted him to do something, he had to do it. He was the youngest child, which meant he always had to do things for the other mice in his family. It got old pretty quickly, but there was nothing Milton could do about it. He just had to accept it.

Most of the time, it just meant helping his parents cook dinner. He never got to do any of the fun parts of cooking. He only ever got to do things like find ingredients in the cupboard or wash the dishes. But still, he was happy to help them cook as long as they made something delicious. Milton didn't think there was anything he loved more than a tasty, hot meal that his parents made.

But that night, his parents weren't making dinner. His grandparents were cooking. Milton figured this meant Grandpa was going to fix up the same yummy beef stew he always made.

Most of the time, everyone in their family got along surprisingly well. A lot of other mice didn't think that would be true since there were so many of them. But actually, since there were so many of them, they had to get along, or else they could never get anything done.

Right now, his grandparents were arguing about what to eat for dinner. This was a strange thing to happen, because it was rare for any argument to happen in the Squeakerton house. His grandfather was saying they should eat beef stew like they always did, but his grandmother was saying that they should start trying out some healthier choices.

This time, his grandfather had already cooked the beef stew, and Milton smelled it from all the way in his room. He didn't want his grandma to win in this argument though, because he didn't like the taste of vegetables.

His parents and grandma were always saying that veggies were good for you, but Milton couldn't stand the taste of them. If his grandma was trying to get the family to eat more healthily, he had to do everything he could stop her from changing the family's menu.

The night after that, he could smell vegetable stew instead of beef stew. She didn't even want to go anywhere near it, so he stayed in his room while everyone else went to go eat dinner.

He heard his grandmother come to his door.

"Milton, are you not feeling well?" She asks him.

"I'm sorry, Grandma, I just don't like to eat vegetables," Milton said.

"You'll like them from the way I could them into the stew, honey. Please give it a try."

But Milton had already tried to make vegetables before, and he didn't want to give them another chance. "It's all right. I can just go without dinner for tonight."

"If you say so," his grandmother said. "I will leave a bowl in your room for you."

As if she hadn't heard what Milton said, Grandma Squeakerton placed a bowl of vegetable stew on his bedside table, and then walked back downstairs where everyone else was having dinner.

He knew he wasn't going to eat it, but Milton liked it over at the soup anyway. There was something about the smell this time that enticed him. He noticed that even though it still had vegetables in it, it still smelled a lot like bed stew.

He had to admit that it smelled really good. He got off his bed and walked up to the stew. He held his nose right over it and took a big, long sniff.

Milton couldn't believe it, but he grabbed the spoon his grandmother gave him and took a bite. Then he took another, and another.

The soup was delicious. He didn't eat any beef in the stew, but he definitely tasted it. He thought to himself that she must have cooked the vegetables in beef even though it didn't have beef in it.

I took a lot of humility, but Milton later admitted to his grandmother that her soup was good. He thought that if healthy food could taste this good, too, he should be eating the healthy stuff.

Even Milton's grandfather had to admit that her soup was tasty, while still having the vegetables they all need. From then on, the Squeakerton family ate Grandma's food for dinner. They did let Grandpa cook for them, too. But when Grandpa cooked, he got a lot of help from Grandma on how to make food that was good for your body, too.

Chapter 7. The Hare Pirates on a Treasure Hunt

It is a beautiful day. There is not a single cloud in the sky far and wide. On the shallow water a pirate ship crosses across the sea.

The sun shines on the sailor. But there is no time for laze. On the ship is once again looking diligently for a treasure island. Because the pirates thirst for gold and jewels.

The helmsman still does not know exactly where the journey should go. Because so far the pirates sail only on the basis of a half treasure map. To find the treasure, you must first look for the other half of the treasure map.

But now there is another problem for now. At the stern of the ship an octopus has settled. That slows down the whole ride. The captain takes a short piece of wood and heads for the octopus. Then he throws the wood as far as he can into the sea. He calls out loud and the octopus jumps from the stern into the water and swims behind the stick. "Well, then you go water-terrier!" The captain whispers in his beard before he goes back to the treasure hunt.

And there it sounds already from the lookout tower: "Land ahead! Hard port! "The captain pushes the helmsman aside and tears the helm around with a grin. In front of them an island appears on the horizon. Is this the Treasure Island? Hard to say without the second part of the map. But it's a start. Hustle is spreading on the pirate ship. The sails are reset quickly. Every hare on board hurries as best he can. Why the rabbits are so hectic you ask?

Well, they are not the only ones looking for the treasure. Other pirates have sneaked the first part of the treasure map and are now looking for wealth and honor.

One evening, the captain's right paw - the lanky Hellgard Hüpfer - was not paying close attention and fell asleep while the treasure map was lying on his bedside table. This moment was maliciously exploited. A devious pirate sneaked into the sleeping chamber of the captain's right paw to secretly draw the treasure map. And now the pirates are in competition with the insidious villains. First come first serve.

True, the Pirates Code does not prohibit treacherously providing an advantage; but he commands the one who finds him first.

The island is getting closer and the lookout is getting loud. "Second part of the treasure map ahead!" Willi gets far-sighted and falls from sheer excitement almost from the observation deck. Phew, that just went well.

When the captain hears the call, he does not trust his eavesdroppers. He rushes to the railing of the pirate ship and reaches for the telescope. "Where? Where? "He exclaims excitedly. But then he sees something that makes his blood freeze in his veins.

The second part of the treasure map is in a bottle post. But this was already fished out of the sea. The captain sees the unbelievable in the distance. "Ai Potz flash. Someone fries an Easter egg for me. This is a Meerjungzibbe holds the Boddel. "Poltert it from the nose of the captain.

And indeed. On the island sits a mermaid, er, sorry, baby boy - as the captain already said - and holds the message in his paws.

There is caution. Because, as the captain already really rumbles on: "With Meerjungzibben is not just cherries eat mi Jung!"

And he orders the sailor to catch up with the sails and slow down.

Then he roars with all his might: "Guns starboard!" All sailors hurry frantically. Then the cannons are dragged to starboard. The sailors sing in rhythm: "And one and draw and one and move ..."

The ship swings from left to right, from right to left. It rocks so hard that some cannons roll back by themselves. "Ai pats again! Just stay a while! "Cries the young Torben dub, as he is pulled by a cannon across the deck.

With all his might he tries to hold the monster. But there is nothing to do. The cannon continues indefatigably on its way. To make matters worse, he stumbles over a plank and flies in a high arc on the rolling cannon.

Now both of them dash past the other pirates with Karacho. Two sailors can take cover at the last moment before the cannon with a bang and the poor Torben dub with a dull - PATSCH - crash against the gang of the ship.

The other sailors can hardly keep from laughing. "That was a clean crash landing, mi Jung! These are cannons and not horses! "The laughter breaks out of the thick pirate Kunjard sausage.

"Well wait," thinks Torben dub and gets up. When he has the cannon back in the right place he deliberately jumps on the tube as if he wants to ride the monster. Then he grabs the fuse, lights the fire and gets ready.

When all the cannons are aligned, the ship is close enough to the island to deliver the first salvo. Now the other pirates ignite the blazing fire and get ready.

"Fire free!" Thundered the captain's powerful voice over the planks. The Lunten are ignited and with a deafening roar hurl the cannon balls from the steel pipes into the open air.

The cannons bounce a bit backwards. Torben dumbs up an arm and yells, "Jiiihah." Sitting on the cannon like a cowboy doing a rodeo.

The other sailors and pirates marvel not bad at the daring pirate boys. Especially not when they see Torben's butt caught fire. Everyone looks at him with big eyes.

Torben himself does not notice and sits proudly like Oskar on the cannon. "N / A? You did not think so, did you? "He boasts. But then he perceives the smell of burnt fur.

He sniffs and sniffs - looks around - and keeps sniffing. "What is it that offends my sense of smell?" He asks when suddenly he discovers the fire on his bottom.

He jumps frantically into the next water barrel. After a loud "Splash Pffffffffff" you can only see steam rising. Soaking wet, the poor dork sits in the barrel. And everyone can laugh heartily again.

In the meantime the mermaid has heard the tremendous bang and jumped in the water. The bottle post with the second part of the treasure map has dropped her.

When the pirate Marla Mutig saw this, she jumped boldly over the plank to get the Boddel. Now she is also spotted by the lookout. "Hare overboard!" Calls Willi Weitsicht just when he suddenly notices that one of the insidious treasure map thieves sneaks over the mainsail.

Down on deck, meanwhile, a large piece of wood is flying past the captain's head. Amazed, he turns around and sees the octopus from earlier. Apparently she has found the stick and wants the captain to throw it again.

Meanwhile, standing on the mast now the rogue with drawn saber directly in front of Willi Weitsicht and mumbled: "I make you shish kebab on the spit." But there it rang from the deck: "Sails clear her water rats!" Bellowed the captain.

He had long since noticed the other pirate ship and does not hesitate to fire long. Immediately the sailors clear the sails and the attacker is swept off the main mast like spinach from the kitchen table. The rogue lands in the sea with a belly slapper.

The octopus jumps happily afterwards. She probably thinks the villain is a stick. You do not want to get stuck in his skin now. It only takes a moment and the rogue flies screaming over the pirate ship. The octopus thought it was too good with the momentum.

After the rogue has flown past the captain, he grabs the telescope and searches in the distance for Marla Mutig in the water. He can not find her.

"Marla come on - where are you? A water rat like you is not drowned, "he whispers to himself. The captain knows they have to hurry if they want to find the treasure first. And there Marla Mutig is his best chance.

The captain can not find the pirate in the water at all. For now she has collected the bottle post and has swum to the island. She just wants to open the message in the bottle when she sees it.

Just within reach, suddenly everything seems in vain. The second part of the map is no longer legible. The mermaid had opened the message in the bottle before leaping into the water. Now the treasure map is saturated with salt water. All the ink has gone and the treasure seems lost.

Marla stares at the card and falls to her knees. Was everything else now? The salt water on the treasure map is now joined by

Marla's tears. She is sobbing and crying. Should everything really be over now?

But as luck would have it, there is a happy ending. Because when Marla looks up, she sees the treasure chest standing right in front of her. The mermaid had already found the treasure. She sat on it just before, without the pirate noticing.

Marla Mutig wipes away her tears and retrieves the golden key from the bottle. Then she puts him in the lock of the chest - the key fits. With a "crack" the lock opens. That's the end of the race - because the Pirate Code rules, who found it first, can keep it.

The captain has now also spotted Marla Mutig and the treasure on the island and shouts to the crew: "We have found the treasure! Today there are carrots for everyone and in abundance! "The pirates jump joyfully up and down.

The insidious villains, however, do not look very happy. According to the Pirate Codex, you lost the race for the treasure. And so they leave untapped things and no prey.

Marla has meanwhile ransacked the treasure chest. The box contains bags of gold, jeweler and jewelry. Most notable, however, is a ring with a diamond twice as large as Marla's paw.

When the other pirates finally reach the island, the joy is still great! It is cheered and celebrated until the sun goes down. Once again a treasure was found. Only the ring with the big diamond has disappeared. Well, who has that?

Chapter 8. The Dream Life

Just when you think life cannot get any worse than it currently is, either something magical can happen that will change your luck or it gets a little bit worse. Those are the only two options, after today you wonder how your luck will go, will it better? Or will your life come crashing down around you? You hear a knock on the door, your tired body drags you to answer it. You open the door to see a business woman, smiling largely as she hands you a heavy briefcase. Puzzled you don't want her to release the case. Who is this woman? Why is she here? Your brain struggles to process this, then she starts talking.

"You are the winner of the dream life sweepstake. You are the luckiest person on Earth right now, and everything is going to change for the better." This feels like a gimmick, surely, she will say you only need to invest, blah, blah, blah. So, you tell her that you are not interested and you just want her to leave you in peace so you can rest. She is dumbfounded as you shut the door in her face. As you walk back to your bed, your phone rings. You answer it to hear a formal voice on the other line announce that he's a lawyer for the World's richest man, a man who died a few weeks ago. In his will he had a list of names, people that he had encountered in his life...everyone from the school librarian in primary school to a drive thru window cashier at the McDonald's. Anyone he met, he added them to this list. Upon his death he wanted his list to become a sweepstakes for his fortune, but his money ruined his life. It tore apart his family, it made him greedy, it made him lazy. He wants someone to be able to live out their dream life, through his will, but with guidance. The lady at the door is the first step towards guiding you to accepting this fortune. After the lawyer explains, you still can't seem to process this. You don't think you met this man, and if you had...would you be so lucky as to win his entire fortune?

Is this that point where your luck changes? Will it be the best thing that ever happened to you? Or will you waste your time? Isn't it worth the amount of time, just to listen to the lady? What harm can it do? You turn around and walk back to the door. Allowing the woman to enter your home. You have a seat at the table and she opens the briefcase. "First, we will start with a questionnaire. I am to guide you to a dream life, not just hand you a fortune. Once that I am certain you are ready to have the fortune, it will be all yours." You hesitantly agree, still feeling this is too good to be true. What is your dream job, do you wish to earn fulfillment through your work, or is it a means to an end? You decide you have nothing to hide from this woman, so you tell her the truth. She nods and moves on to the next question.

What is your dream family? Do you have it? Would money change your family, for the better or for the worse?

If you could live anywhere in the world, where would you live? Why would you live there?

"Ok, that takes care of the basics. Give me a few moments and I'll be back soon." As she leaves the room, you suddenly find yourself a bundle of nerves. Your body is tense and achy. You want to relax yourself, not let this work you up. So, you take a deep breath in as you stretch and flex the muscles in your body. As you exhale slowly, you allow the muscles to relax. You can feel a warm tingling sensation rushing through as you repeat the process. You keep breathing in slowly, becoming aware of your body. It is heavy and tired, you relax into the chair and focus on the simple task of breathing and allowing your body to rest. The lady enters the room again and you feel relaxed, maybe this is for the best. "Now, we will start building your dream life. Starting with some major purchases, then working through the minor ones so we can organize your new life. What type of car do you wish to have? Do you need anything custom on it?" She hands you a form, as you order your dream car.

You think about all the cars you've wanted throughout your life, until you finally settle on one. You try to keep in mind, this is because you're not spending your own money. This is just a 'dream' car for a reason. Think of every elaborate detail you would want in that car, including a personal driver, if that's what you want. Once you have etched every detail into that paper, hand it back to her.

"Now, we can decide on your land. I got some listings in the areas you described as your dream location. Please, look over these and see if any of them are what you had in mind."

As you look through the real estate listings, you see so many perfect opportunities. They are exactly where you would want to build a dream home. You look at the surrounding areas and you can picture the beautiful landscape now. Hearing the local noises. Smelling the scents, feeling the peace it would bring to you to be there now. You realize you've held onto this particular listing for a while. You let her know this is the one you like the most. Her fingers fly across her phone as she informs you that the land now belongs to you. All the paperwork will be signed at the end. You are dumbfounded as you look at her and ask, "Why me? How did I know this man, why would he want to give me this dream life?"

"I don't know the details. I just know that your name was on his list, and it is the name that was selected. My job is planned out in exquisite details, which is why we are able to shuffle along through these tasks. You are in fact a very lucky person, with a great fortune. Let's not lose momentum now, the sooner we have everything in order, the sooner you get to experience your dream life. The best contractor and his team are prepared to draw up your dream house when you are ready. They will be here shortly, I have just sent them the land, so they will have a better idea on how to make things work for you. While we wait for them, are you happy in your current dwellings? Or do you want a new temporary home while your dream home is being constructed?"

You think long and hard on the question. Now that money is apparently not a problem, what do you want to do while your dream home is being constructed? Do you want to live here and just wait? Do you want to hire movers and move into a nice upscale place? Or a place far away from everyone and everything while you process your new life? Surely, you'll want to escape the media, if you stay in your current dwellings, you need people to help keep the media off you. Or maybe you'll step into the spotlight and shine, embracing your dream life. When you thought of what you wanted you let the lady know and she assures you that nothing will be a problem. All your wishes for your new life will be answered. The contractor has arrived with his team, only now that it is not just this lady in front of you, or the voice on the phone from earlier, the reality is really sinking in. Your life is going to become everything you've ever wanted. As they bring in their things and get settled you start to wonder what you will do with your life? With all your worries fading quicker and quicker into your past, what does your soul want? When everything material in this world becomes easily bought, what are the things you need to work on? How can you be the person that you truly want to be? Do you need all this money to accomplish your goals? Will it make your life that much easier? Probably, but when all those little inconveniences are covered, and no longer troublesome, does your life feel empty or is there a vast opening that you can now explore? Will you travel the world? Will you fund new charities or help those already established? The contractor introduces himself and starts to ask questions about your dream home so that they may begin the process...you feel your mind flood with images of beautiful houses, but you don't know where to start. You inhale and exhale and decide right now to start becoming the new you, as you describe this home. This home reflects who you are as a person. Build it from the ground up. Describe how you want your base, in detail, build your dream home, until you drift into a deep peaceful rest. When you wake up tomorrow, you will be this new person with a strong base to work on your dream life.

Chapter 9. Apollo's blazing Sun

Once upon a time, long, long ago, there lived a beautiful, brilliant man. He lived atop his mountain, singing songs and enjoying the world, and doing all of his very important jobs that he had. But when spring was done, he would come out to play his favorite and his most important job of all. His name was Apollo—he was the ruler of the sun, and he was responsible for making sure that it came and went every day.

Apollo was the most handsome man, some people said. He had beautiful golden hair and wonderful blue eyes. No matter how long he went, he never grew a beard, and his hair curled nicely around his face. His body was very muscular and strong, thanks to his work that he had to do, and he was very strong. Everyone that saw him would declare just how beautiful he is.

But, he was more than just a pretty face. He was very important. He handled many different important jobs. He was supposed to guide the sun through the sky, and he tried to do so the best that he could, but he had so many other jobs, that sometimes, he did a little less and sometimes, more. He was supposed to bring with him healing to the world—he helped people who had become ill so they could recover and begin to feel better again, and he loved that he did so. He was the ruler of music and poetry, and he loved to treat the world to the sounds of his beautiful golden lyre. He was the ruler of archery and he had to help people's arrows fly straight and far. He was the ruler of the herds of farmers, and the protector of the young, born under Gaia's reign during the spring.

As you can imagine, Apollo was a very busy man. He always had a lot to do during his time out and about. He had to make sure that people got better when they were sick. He had to make sure that the sun was in the sky long enough for the plants to grow. He had to keep his eye on the sheep and cows of the people. It was a very busy job, but he would not have it any other way. He loved that he had to help the world grow. He loved that it was his job to help the plants thrive around him. He loved that under his rule, the days grew warmer and the plants grew taller and taller.

Sometimes, during the winter, he grew slower with his job and he would come out less and less. But, this was not because he was slacking—but rather, Apollo had many different important jobs. One of his very important jobs is to heal. He has to help people heal from their illnesses every winter, so he has even less time than usual to keep the sun in line because he is too busy helping everyone that gets sick in the winter.

Every winter, Apollo goes out bravely. He sees people that are sick and he tries to help them. He brings with him the power to heal and the energy that they need to help themselves to recover from whatever it was that has made them ill. He brings with him the warmth and comfort that they need to feel better again, and as he is there, trying to make people feel healthier again, he is busy. His sun does not stay up in the sky as long because he cannot hold it up as long when he is busy trying to help so many people, and more people get sick when it is winter.

But, soon, every spring, Gaia appears. Gaia starts to thaw out the frozen earth. Gaia starts to bring with her more health and good fortune. Gaia helps Apollo because less people get sick when she is there, bringing life to the world. And it is then, when Gaia starts to help the world that Apollo gets to spend less time with the people that are sick and more time helping the sun. It is when spring thaws out the earth that Apollo can begin to warm it up even more.

Every spring, Apollo would see Gaia working hard. He would see her preparing the world to grow and he would know that he had to help. Those plants that Gaia was sowing into the ground could not grow just on magic itself—rather, they needed more help than that! They also needed sunlight and warmth to help them grow as big and strong as they could to prepare for the autumn harvest. But, just like the plants, you also need the summer sun to grow as well.

The sunlight in summer is very healthy for you. It helps your body to produce enough of the very special vitamins that you need. The sun can help make sure that your moods are good and happy. The sun can help you learn to enjoy the time that you are out and have fun playing! It can also help you to grow your own plants in your own garden, just like Gaia did. The summer is a very important time of growing for all creatures.

The creatures that were born in the spring begin to grow up during this time. Birds leave their nests and fly away to be on their own. Caterpillars are able to hide away in their chrysalises and go through that wonderful metamorphosis that will help them to become the wondrous and beautiful and mysterious butterflies that they can grow into. The baby animals all start to grow and become more confident, and they all have plenty of food to eat, thanks to Gaia's gift to the world and Apollos' brave and strong effort that he put into bringing the sun into the sky.

During the summer, while Apollo holds the sun into the air for longer, he brings with him a beautiful, golden lyre. The lyre makes the most wonderful sound that anyone has ever heard—it is more beautiful than the sounds of the birds singing in the warm summer breeze, and more beautiful than the whisper of the wind through the leaves and the grass. It is more beautiful than the sounds of the crickets chirping and the cicadas buzzing away. The sound that his lyre makes is so beautiful that all who hear it must cry, for they have never heard anything so wondrous.

Apollo brings with him many more gifts. What can you do when you have more daylight? What happens when your days grow longer? Grown-ups have more time that they could use to grow all of that very important food, but what about you? Some children, in the summertime, love to go swimming in the cool water. Swimming is fun—but have you ever thought of going swimming outside in the winter?

No!! It would be too cold. But, because Apollo is there, playing his beautiful golden lyre and making sure that he is paying very close attention to the sun to allow it to stay out for much longer in order to help his friend, Gaia, you know that the weather is warmer. You know that it is okay to go swimming and enjoy the great, warm sun above you. You know that it is okay to enjoy the outdoors, because you do not have to worry about how cold it is. You do not have to worry about your plants dying or freezing. You do not have to worry about snow burying everything around you. Instead, you can play out without jackets on! You can enjoy the sunshine! You can sing a song underneath the blazing sun that Apollo is holding just for you.

Remember, even when you feel like the sun is too hot, and in the summertime, sometimes it is, that sunlight and that heat is actually doing a very important job. It is helping the world around you. It is making sure that there will be enough food for everyone to harvest in the autumn to live in the winter, when the snow is on the ground and it is too cold to grow anything. Remember that summer is a period of growth. Just as spring is rebirth, summer represents a time when everything around you is growing very quickly. The world is thriving underneath Apollo's blazing sun. The leaves in the trees become bushier and greener, and they can make more air for you to breathe. The grass that the cows will eat grows thicker than ever and they get to eat it all up when they need it the most! The animals all around you will all get everything they need thanks to Apollo.

And, because the animals and the plants around you get everything that they need, you get what you need as well. So, the next time that you feel like it is too hot outside or you feel like you are getting grumpy under the heat of the sun, remember something: Apollo is doing you a great favor. He is doing the whole world a great favor. While Gaia plants the seed with her beautiful dance, Apollo helps it to grow and flourish. Instead of being upset or angry about the warmth, what if you stopped and told yourself that it was actually a wonderful thing? What if you reminded yourself that the sun is a gift? What if you reminded yourself that the beautiful light that the sun, thanks to Apollo, gives you is really there to help you?

And, what if you decided that you wanted to help Apollo, too? What if you did your part to help nurture all of the plants that grow in your home? What if you helped to bring them water, for even though the plants love the sun and they need it to be bright and warm so they can grow, the plants also need water? You can become a helper of Apollo. You can become a helper to the plants and to the summer. You can help the world around you grow. And, as the summer draws to an end and the plants are all grown up, Apollo, very tired after a summer of very heavy lifting of the sun, begins to let the sun stay up for less and less time. He begins to let the sun fall down sooner. He lets the earth begin to chill. He lets the world begin to cool down once more, and soon, autumn, and before long, Demeter will appear to guide the world from a stage of growth to one of harvest to prepare for the cold, long winter.

Chapter 10. The Genius

Tonight, we are going to witness the power of the human mind. An extraordinary existence that lies within you and the power within it has so much untapped potential. We are going to tap into that genius potential to give you the most relaxing and serene peace that your body and mind have ever experienced. First, you must clear your mind. Let's do this with an organizational approach. Imagine a room; it can be stark white, it can be an ordinary office; maybe it's a storage room, or an extraterrestrial room that is dark with sleek modern touches. This room will be your way to file and organize your thoughts, putting them away for the night.

Let us start collecting those thoughts, by exploring your thought superhighway and gathering everything we can find. Collect the thoughts however you need; if they are organized maybe you can set up a roadblock. Position yourself to slow, then halt the thoughts, processing which way they need to go. Compressing the thoughts into tiny manageable pieces. Maybe your thoughts are scattered, you can lay a net or a trap, and gather them all up at once? Then take each thought, figure out what it is, assign it to a file. As all the thoughts ramble and bounce around in your mind, stop them and gather them into a pile. Maybe some thoughts are linked together, place them within the same file or box; however big you need that storage bin or containment system to be. Your stack is growing higher and higher as all the thoughts from the day leave your thought highway and go into your manageable file system.

Once you have a hefty pile, you lift it up. The weight feeling like a burden and weighing you down, you take the thoughts to your organizational room. Let's begin filing away these thoughts. Stacking them, filing them, whatever you need to do to clean up your mind space. Making things nice, tidy, and neat. Take your time, go through every thought, making sure it is tucked away, not going to fall off and ramble its way back onto the thought highway. If you feel any loose thoughts escaping, making their way back onto the thought highway, let it go, don't fight it. Finish putting away what you have now, these thoughts are ready to be put to rest. Once everything is put in its place, go back to the highway for a last sweep. Any errant thoughts can be grabbed up now. Catch those thoughts and take them back to the organization room. Are all your thoughts tucked away? If yes, your mind is blank and ready to explore? If not, take a moment and keep collecting and storing until you're ready to move on.

You leave the organization room behind you now. You travel through your mind, we're going to tap into the parts you do not use often enough. You can visualize your brain, the parts you use often are alive and electric. As you pass these parts by, allow them to calm down. Let them rest, they have done enough for today, we don't need them for what we are going to do. You pass by the central part, the one that controls your breathing, your heart rate, gently caress it. Let it know it can relax too, it can slow down. Feel your breathing calm, your heart rate a soft cadence; the reassurance that life is within you and will continue to be so in the morning. As you feel your mind relaxing you continue to travel through. Passing the parts, you do not use enough, seeing them with their soft warm glow, welcoming you to tap into them. Once you have located the untapped potential, touch it. Reach up your arms and stretch them long. Stretch your torso and back, twist to reach it. Make your legs long all the way to your toes. Now you feel it, you're touching this dull area and a warm sensation is starting to come alive and you can feel it washing over you. It starts to warm up and emit a little happy glow that travels all through your body. Your muscles start to relax as the warmness caress it, your mind feels pleasant, bubbling and cloudy, until it sinks into the warm, soft light, then you can see a vivid green field all around you.

The sky is blue, the tall grass, soft and green. Your entire body feels warm and relaxed. Let's see if this is the true potential of your mind with a little test. Imagine yellow dandelions growing all over the field. Big ones, small ones. Count them as you add the yellow dandelions, until you can't count. There's too many, millions and millions of yellow flowers surrounding you with happiness and joy. This is the power of your mind, if your mind isn't cooperating then you're not ready for this area. Don't give up, go back, explore your brain, find another untapped area and keep trying. You will find one that will let you explore. Once you're in a warm area and you see the field that you can control, you are there. Now that we are all there let's practice this new and pleasing sensation of control, turn the dandelions into their fluffy white flowers, ready to release their seeds into the world. All around you, in a field full of white fluffy dandelions. Pick one up. Take a deep breath in, then blow it out slowly. Watching the seeds spiral from the flower into the air. As the seeds float back to the earth, steady yourself. This is just a very small power that rests inside you, it can do so much more. Take another deep breath in as you pick another dandelion. Exhale as you blow those seeds and come to terms with the fact you are a genius. You are capable of anything you set your mind to. Rest and relaxation can help you tap into that genius.

You command your mind and body. Right now, you command them to relax. Your entire body is soft, relaxed, and pliable. Your mind is warm, enriched, and welcoming to the thoughts of your tapped genius potential. You can go anywhere in the world right now, without leaving this state of relaxation. Where do you want to go? Picture that place; is it an ocean shore, a busy city, a small village, or a place you know well? What does it smell like? What can you hear? What can you see? How does it make you feel? Take a moment and enjoy this place, explore the sensations. Is it everything you hoped it would be?

This is your mind allowing you to experience the most wonderful sensations whenever you want it to. This power is incredible. You want to be on a beach in Greece, done. You want to be in the mountains in Asia, done. You want to be anywhere in space or time, you can do that. You are a wonderful, amazing creature, with limitless abilities as you bring yourself into ultimate relaxation at the same time. Would you like to see what else your mind is capable of?

Picture the tallest building in the world. Now get to the top of it. How does your mind get you there? Do you instantly appear on the top of the building? Do you walk up to the building, enter, and take an elevator? Do you start the arduous task of climbing the stairs? Do you gear up and climb the side of the building? Or maybe you come from above, using a parachute as you fall from a plane to land on top of the tallest building in the world. So many possibilities can spring from one simple suggestion. If you can get to the top of this building, then you can do anything. Take your time, or get it done quickly. It doesn't matter, because all the potential to do it, is inside your mind.

Can you understand now how beautiful and creative your mind is? Your mind can grow and continue to astound you every day, if you let it. Listen to your mind, let it guide you... Let your mind connect with your heart, picture the direct link between the two. This connection will know what you want the most in this life. Do not stop it, do not slow it down. Let it carry you away, showing you your hopes and dreams and how you can achieve them. Stay in this state of relaxation, do not let the errant thoughts break out of their storage room. They are locked away, stored nice and neatly for tomorrow. Tonight, is not about any of those thoughts, quickly lock that door, and then forget it. It is about you, who you are, what you want, and how you are going to get it.

Everything becomes clear and easy to manage. Just like organizing your thoughts, your mind can control and process anything you bring its way. Let it take over, just as it took you into this deep relaxation. Once you are in total control of your mind, then you can shut it down and go to sleep. Enjoy your peaceful rest, and I look forward to seeing your genius potential in the world.

Chapter 11. Crystal Cave

I have always had this fascination with cold and dark places. Some people are drawn like moths toward all things light and traditionally beautiful, but that just isn't me. It hasn't ever been me. I love Victorian architecture and the way that the moon looks when it is pumped and hung high in the night sky. I am not othering myself from the rest of the population, but I am here to proclaim that we are here, and we exist. Beauty is in the eye of the beholder. In this case, the beholder was an ice queen.

My friends and I decided that we would take a trip through Europe. We would be going through Asia the year after that. We would continue until we had covered as much area as we possibly could. To my delight, I was allowed to select some of the places that we visited. There were interesting castles and old churches. I could have asked for a better group of people with which to travel.

When one of my friends suggested Iceland, I was initially hesitant. I had just never invested enough time to really get to know the culture and the people, or I would have been thrilled. It turned out to be such an interesting and culturally rich place. We didn't meet one single dour person on the whole stop. Iceland spoke to my soul in a way that no other place had.

My first experience was the plane landing during an overcast day. The sky was beautiful and foggy grey. We walked among the streets of Reykjavik, passing all the dimly lit shops. It was a long stretch of flickering lights. It was frigid, and everyone was in a hurry to get where they were going. I had not felt cold like this in a few weeks. It settled in my bones, and my body seemed to shake and rattle against itself. Lovers on the street pulled themselves closer to try and fight against the icy air.

Grated, the air was not cold enough to warrant the name Iceland, but at least Chillyland. We had decided to go in the depths of winter, which is maybe not the best time to tour anything. The whole atmosphere was made for me though. It was dark, beautiful and grey.

We found some familiar food on the main street. We had hotdogs for dinner as we continued our exploration. We eventually managed to find a tourism center that had information about places that we should try to see on our trip. I browsed through the pamphlets with my friends. One of them jokingly pointed out that we should go and see the Crystal Caves for me. To her surprise, the idea was a hit with everyone. We paid for a hotel for the night and decided that we would set out in search of the caves tomorrow. We all mused back and forth to one another about the adventures of our trip so far. I sipped a hot chocolate by the window watching as the locals continued on about their business on the street below.

The experience was so much more than I was expecting. The inside of the cave was like landing on the moon. There was a faint azure glow that cast itself all along the inside. It looked ghostly and surreal, and it seemed to go on forever.

The rock and ice twisted and turned in on itself. The echo inside the caves was also something totally unique to that experience. It was positively gothic and breathtaking. We were all very cold, but the possibility of pushing further into the cave was a good motivator to ignore the temperature. We all said that when we left, the first thing we would do would be to find a nice hot drink to warm our souls.

The ice was edgy and somehow delicate. It was absolutely beautiful. We were covered in heavy gear that allowed us to explore. We had to enter through what seemed like a hole in the snow. For all of the stillness and tranquility of the cave, it was also dangerous in some ways.

The cave was a mix of ice and rock. There were tunnels and large caverns all around us. It was all cast in that same blue light. The floor seemed to be mostly rock and gravel. There was also a place where we were required to sit on the ice and slide through a hole. Our guide showed us the correct way to get down and then assured that everyone made it to the other side.

There were places that were wide open and also placed where the ice was almost closing in on us. It was one of the most magical things that I have ever seen. I see those caves when I am dreaming. It was an otherworldly wonderland. I cannot wait for my chance to return again. I felt very proud of finally having met my soulmate in a travel destination.

Chapter 12. Demeter's Duty

Once upon a time, long, long ago, there was a beautiful woman named Demeter. Demeter had a very important duty, for she was responsible for making sure that, every autumn, as the leaves turn yellow and brown, that there was enough of a harvest for the humans to eat. She took this job very seriously, and every year, as the days began to grow shorter again, she would work very hard. She would go from crop to crop, touching each and every one to bring it to the perfect ripeness. Oftentimes, she would travel along with her daughter, Persephone, and together, they would touch the plants to ensure that the humans were fed. They knew that they had to work hard if they wanted to take care of the people, and the people knew that they were taken care of by their kind and loving goddess, Demeter.

It was inevitable—every year, as Apollo grew tired from holding up the sun, and as Apollo grew busier and busier, and therefore had to leave the sunlight of summer behind, and the plants were fully grown, it was only natural that Demeter, the queen over the harvest, would come by. When the plants were grown as much as they could be, there was nothing left for them to do! They could not be left on the vines, and they would not make it through the winter if they were not helped in some way! The green leaves of the trees would freeze if they were left on the trees, and they would become damaged. The wheat needed to be dried so it could be saved for later. The apples need to be perfectly ripe so they could be picked and saved. She was welcomed greatly by people everywhere, and even though with her touch and ripening of all of the food around her, she brought the winds that Boreas would fly on, too, she was loved by all.

Everyone loved Demeter, and Demeter loved them all, too. She was known to be fair and just. She was known to be kind. She was like a mother to everyone, making sure that everyone had the food that they would need, and as she did so, she made the trees and their leaves change colors. She made the crops grow into beautiful harvests. Her very favorite crop of them all was the corn that she would carefully ripen. She would go to each and every single ear of corn, and she would touch them all, gently running her fingers over their kernels, and as she did so, she would see them all turn the perfect shade of yellow.

They had to be just right, so when the people picked them, they could be saved for later, Demeter would always tell her daughter as she picked up the next one, and the next one, and the one after that. She was very thorough and she never missed a single kernel, even though she would work so hard that she would go and sleep all winter long.

"Why do you spend so much time on all of that, Mama?" asked Persephone one day, watching carefully as Demeter lovingly touched each kernel. "Couldn't you just do it quickly and not worry about it all so much?" She knew that her mother was very busy, for her mother would not sleep during this time. She would spend every moment of the autumn months, preparing the whole wide world for the winter and working very hard to make sure that, at the end of the day, they would be able to protect all of the plants, and all of the people. Demeter was a very kind and loving goddess and she wanted more than anything else in the world to ensure that each and every plant, no matter how big or small, was prepared for the winter. She wanted to make sure that all of the plants could be harvested and saved for the people to eat when the earth was frozen and nothing grew around her.

"Because, my child," said Demeter, as she looked over the corn, inspecting it carefully to make sure that she had done a good job, "It is my duty. We all have duties that we must fill, as sure as the seasons are. Just as we have winter, spring, summer, and autumn, we must all do our rightful duty to ensure that the seasons pass as they should. It is our duty to protect the people of this great land and it is our duty to make sure that, at the end of the day, we work very hard to give them what they need, for without them, what are we?" Demeter believed that it was her job to make sure that everyone was cared for. She viewed every god or goddess as responsible for taking care of all of the people of the world, as it was their job. They controlled everything, from the weather to the days. They controlled how long the sun was up and how long the sun was down. They controlled the way the wind blew and when the seasons changed, and because of that, she was certain of one thing, and one thing alone: She would make sure that every autumn, she did her best to prepare.

This meant that the winds would grow colder. This was not because she was a cold person, but because she believed that if the weather got colder little by little, instead of suddenly, the people would be able to tolerate it better. This meant that leaves fell—but this was not a sign of the trees dying, but rather, a sign that they would live again! The tree was going to conserve its energy and sleep! This meant that the corn would dry up—but not to starve the people; rather, it would bring them a food that they could save all winter long and eat all winter long.

Persephone listened very closely to what her mother had to say, for she often went out to help Gaia with the thawing of the Earth after Boreas leaves the land. Persephone knew that it was her job to help wake the Earth up. But, unlike Persephone, Demeter had a very different job. Demeter's job was to help the Earth go to sleep, and Demeter liked to do that job as carefully and diligently as she could. But, Demeter was not cruel. She was not harsh or unloving; she was very motherly and she cared very deeply for everyone.

So, the next time that you go outside on that crisp autumn morning and feel disappointed that the leaves are falling down off of the trees and the wind is getting chillier, do not fret— rather, rejoice in what you know! Rejoice in the fact that, at the end of the day, you know that Demeter, and all of her friends, are there helping you with the world around you. You need to have autumn, a period of rest and relaxation and preparation for the world. It is a time in which the world begins to slow down.

Animals settle down to hunker for the winter. Plants begin to prepare to make it through a winter without being hurt by freezing. It is a time in which the animals prepare to sleep. It is like your very own special, personal bedtime routine, but, instead of your mother or father reading you a story, Demeter is reading as a story to the plants and animals of the world. She is working hard to protect everyone and everything. She is trying her best to make sure that she can help each plant finish up and get some rest, and in doing so, she is trying her best to make sure that the people have what they need.

Remember, this too will pass. Soon, Demeter's own duty will be wrapped up. Soon, she will be done with the harvest. She will finish making sure that every single plant is ready to be harvested. Demeter's own duties to slow down, to relax, to preserve, will slow down and she will retire for the season, just like the rest of her friends. She and Persephone will go back to their homes and wait out the next time that they are needed, and when they are needed, they will go right back to meeting their duties. They will be right back to business, for that is their job and they take their jobs very seriously.

Do not forget that, as the leaves yellow and dry and fall to the ground, you should rejoice; you should remember to be grateful for the year that you have had. You should remember that, at the end of the day, you were given a whole year to play and grow and thrive. Your plants were planted and grew and matured. The seeds turned into plants, and then into flowers and fruit. But, with all cycles, there comes a time that the cycle has to start slowing down. There comes a time in which the cycle needs to begin to reset, and Demeter's autumn and Demeter's time of harvest are exactly that.

Chapter 13. A Walk through the Clearing

I don't know how long I had been walking for, but I was sure that I must be almost there. My friend said it would take an hour or so to get to the clearing, but I had budgeted for two hours because I knew I wanted to take my time walking. I hadn't brought a watch with me, but judging by how far the sun had moved since I started, I was sure it had been nearly two hours at this point. I felt the crunching of the gravel under my feet as I continued to follow the marked trail, and took my time in admiring the sights around me. Luscious greenery adorned the path on either side and every now and again, I would see a squirrel or a bird flutter away from the path and into the trees to avoid being seen by me. Of course, I would always pause and watch, enjoying the experience of being alone in the forest with these beautiful creatures.

As I continued walking, I could see the path beginning to widen up ahead. In the distance, I could hear the gentle rushing of water and I knew that I had arrived where I was meant to. Despite how excited I was, I slowed my pace even more, wanting to take in all of the sights that were arising before me. After a long, hard year of going through many of life's trials and tribulations, this was my first true break alone and I did not want to waste it worrying or drowning in overwhelm of my reality. I paused for a moment and breathed in deeply, smelling the green air from the fresh forestry around me. I sighed, feeling the sun shining against my back as it continued to rise through the sky. It must have been around 11:30 AM, as I had hit the trail around 9:30 AM. The heat of the sun was beginning to grow warmer and the forest was slowly drying out for the day as the dew from the night before began to evaporate. I took another step forward, and then another, allowing the lull of the waterfall's sweet sound to draw me forward. As I did, the view of the clearing began to open in front of me.

The clearing was just as my friend had described it: there was a large grassy patch with a crystal clear body of water off to the right side. The trees grew around the edges of the grass, yet not too close to the waterfall. There was plenty of space to enjoy the view, or get into the waterfall should I desire. Around the edges of the waterfall, the trees rose high, although none were taller than the peak of the waterfall itself. The waterfall fell down from a sheer cliff, which clearly had trees lining the falling body of water on either side at the top as well. The clearing felt cozy, almost like a small den that had been carved out of the vast forest.

I walked closer to the waterfall, and as I did, I could see the frothy bubbles foaming around the water from where the waterfall was rushing into it. As I reached the water, I noticed footprints were still formed in the sand at the edges of the water from people who had been there recently and I felt a sense of comfort in knowing that this space was enjoyed by many. I, too, slipped my own shoes off and followed the footprints, walking around the edge of the water and finding myself next to the cliff, looking in behind the waterfall itself. There, a moist rock wall that had been smoothed by the moving water stood tall and strong. I admired the way the water looked and wondered if anyone had ever crawled in there before to see the water from the back. I gazed at the trail that may lead there, but decided against it as I worried it may be too difficult for me to do on my own, and knew that I was alone so if I needed help I would be in trouble. After a few more moments, I turned around and saw the lush green grass behind me, and gazed out into the clearing from the opposite angle from where I had walked in from. I followed my footprints back toward my shoes, taking my time and feeling the moist ground beneath my feet. The sun continued to shine down over the clearing, and I could feel it growing warmer with every passing moment.

When I reached my shoes again, I turned back toward the water and began breathing in deeply, and exhaling all of my breath as much as I could. I sat down and dipped my toes into the edge of the water, feeling how cool it was against my skin, and meditating on the sensation of peace that was wrapped all around me. As I looked into the water, I could not help but notice how grateful I was for some clarity in my life, even if that clarity was merely the clear water at the edge of the waterfall. I looked up into the waterfall itself and saw how the water was white with fury from rushing off the edge of the cliff so fast, and paused for a moment to reflect on the lesson before me. That was, no matter how chaotic things may get, and no matter how fast, hard, or long we may fall for, there is always the potential that we may end up resting at the edge of calmness after our journey. I realized there was no reason for me to hold so tightly to my stresses and worries when I could just as easily relax into the moment and trust that in the end, I could find my calmness once more.

Chapter 14. The Taxi to Nowhere

It is nighttime, it seems like it has been forever. You are in the backseat of a car, with a blanket, and you are very, very comfortable. The car vibrates softly on the road. It seems to be going at a good and consistent speed. Every once in a while, it will rock itself to a top, sweetly, then hum back along until it reaches another steady speed for a good long while. Who is driving? You don't know. You see the back of his head. It is a warm, friendly looking man. He is calm and still and has his eyes on the road. Where are you going? You don't remember. You had some destination in mind. It occurs to you, you are in a taxi, a taxi that was called for you. Wherever you are going, you know it is a safe destination, and where you are meant to be. However long it takes for you to get there, you will be comfortable, and you will be safe, and, you feel, the longer it takes, the better, because here, where you are now, is some kind of paradise, totally calm, and safe, and secure, and still, and alone, in this backseat. If you were to look up in the rearview mirror of the front seat, you would see the driver notice your gaze and match it, and give a warm, affectionate smile, then avert his eyes back to the road. There is no nervous, idle chit chat in this peaceful environment. There is an unspoken bond between you and the driver, a bond of the heart, and you both are so comfortable with each other you might as well not even be separate beings. He knows where you are going, and he is taking you there, and you are as safe in his hands as you would be in your own, so it is now allowed for you to totally relax and pay absolutely no mind to anything. There is nothing else. Whatever worries existed in life outside of this taxi; they are neither here nor there. You are going to your destination, and on this long, safe trip through eternal night, you have absolutely nothing to worry about that has not already been taken care of. You do not have a seatbelt on, because that is how safe you are. You are laying back against the right backseat door, with a very comfortable pillow, cuddled up in the world's fluffiest, richest, warmest blanket. It seems as if it is very cold outside the taxi, maybe even a little chilly inside of it, as you can feel on your face, the only exposed skin outside of the blanket. You can see the frost and condensation on the windows of the taxi, slow drips of frosty water going from the top to the bottom, slightly curved back by the momentum of the moving vehicle, then many more taking their place. There might even be a light hint of snow, few and far between flakes dusting down and providing a light accouterment to the pitch-blackness of the sky, but you are so drowsy, and so relaxed, and you don't even bother to tell for sure. No buildings are present from the low angle you are seeing out the window, all though there might be many slightly below, but you do see the occasional calming orange glow of a streetlight. And beyond these gothic lanterns your attention is drawn to the infinite array of stars. There are more stars than you have ever seen, big and small, bright and beautiful, yet so very, very far away. Just, to you, now, a calm reminder of life far away from this planet, from yourself, life going on and on; infinity. Far away from you, you begin to make out the static sounds of what might be a highway, the low buzzing drone of many, many cars going many, many places, so far away, so apart from you. It is incredibly soothing, like some low and consistent heartbeat of the world. You are just one traveler, in the veins, going where you are going, and it feels so peaceful to you to just become that one part in a sea of infinite parts, doing what you are doing, being who you are, simply existing, as the world exists around you. The infinite night, the constant wee hours of the morning, you zoned out a long time ago into this peaceful, blissful state and you aren't really sure how long you have been in the backseat of this taxi since you even noticed that you were. And if that were to be defined, then how long before that. It seems circular, like you might have just been a passenger in the backseat of this taxi, nestled up in this blanket, protected from the elements, warm, but so alive, forever. For all you know, this could just be life; calm, quiet, consistent, relaxed, for eternity. You lose focus on any one particular thing, and, though your eyes are still open, you don't really know what you are looking at; just blackness, the pitch-blackness of this eternal night, where you are a passenger. The hum of the heartbeat of the world takes over, and your body relaxes into a state in which you begin to leave it and become everyone and everything, everywhere, going wherever. Somewhere, sometime, the taxi driver flips on the warm signal of the radio, AM, and it is just one more beautiful layer of white noise atop the infinite. You hear, somewhere, voices talking, and music existing upon music in the backgrounds of our souls. In this warm cocoon, the infinite layers of life dance into oblivion all around you, and you are succumbed, in glorious awe, totally relaxed, and tranquil, and entranced in its hypnotic beauty. Lifetimes must pass, as they always do, in this backseat, with you as a passenger going somewhere, anywhere, to your destination. The heartbeat of the world and the hum of the radio and the steady, consistent, non-stop calm rumble of the taxi on your whole body begin to become one sensation, the buzzing of the world soul, the eternal drone. You are what you are, going where you are going, and you become this, and all that you are drifts away, and there is nothing, and you are asleep.

Chapter 15. Becoming the Orb

You are in the middle of a valley, at dusk, the sun setting behind the mountains, the warm pink and golden glow barely rising above the peaks. The air is heavy with moisture, as if stuck in eternal half-rain, water falling down forever from the sky in a fine mist. There is electricity in the sky, like lightning might strike at any moment, thunder rumbling in the distance, purple clouds racing across, from mountain to mountain. You are cross-legged, meditative, hands placed palms-up on your knees, back straight, nostrils opened, and you close your eyes. Within you, the entire scene is inverted down to your core. The pink and gold of the skyline glows down to your depths. The moisture dances through your entire physiology, down to your core. The thunder rumbles somewhere down below, in the furthest reaches, and the threat of a lightning storm is imminent, inside. You sit and watch the weather in your being, both inside and outside of you. You see all there is to see, within yourself. Suddenly, the landscape outside ceases to exist, existing only within you, and, as it disappears, a golden ball, just a pinpoint, appears in the middle of this internal scene. It is right in the center of your solar plexus. You gaze upon it, and touch it. It is a blinding light, the likes of which you have never seen. It is somewhat terrifying, awe-inspiring, but calming. You are ready for this small light to do whatever it is that it is going to do, with or without you. Slowly, steadily, it begins to grow, as it grows, like a seismic wave, it silences the entire environment, there is nothing that is not silent, and still, besides this growing orb. It grows, and grows. It has overcome your entire body now, which has shut off completely, and is now growing through it, out of the skin. As it grows, your awareness grows with the ball, out of your body, and your body becomes a thing of the past, eaten alive by the ball, lost deep within. When the ball is big enough, its surface touches the ground, and continues to grow through it. It is now through the grass, within the dirt, and still growing, outwards, and upwards, and down below where you can see. Everything is bleeding into this ball as if being pulled magnetically, while the ball, in turn, is sucking in and pulling outwards. Trees, and bushes, small creeks, all manner of plant life and animal life, within the ball, until it has swallowed up the entire valley, and half the sky. And it continues onto the mountains, devouring them, slowly, the mountains welcoming their descent into this golden glow. The clouds, as well, are assimilated into this light. Eventually, the glow of the sunset itself is no longer differentiable from the orb, becoming brighter in the orb as the orb is brighter than it. Slowly the mountains beside the mountains are embraced, then the next, and the next, until half the range is taken, then the whole range, miles and miles and still growing. Somewhere within is where you are, yet you are the whole, growing outwards. The entire mountain range is taken, and down the foothills, everything, all life, all the rivers, all the waters, all the people, and the places, and things, over a whole city, a whole county, a whole population, a whole state. Now, the orb devours entire cities. All the electricity in the cities, all the lights, and the sounds, and the traffic, and the energy, is muted in comparison with the infinite energy of this orb. However wild, and insane, and gigantic whatever the orb takes, it becomes nothing inside the orb, for the orb itself has already maxed out the energies within, and in it all things, so as to make everything it touches not whatever it is, but all things as well. And with it, you continue to grow. You are now the cities, and the states, and the countries. There is now an entire country within the orb, and an entire atmosphere, up into space, and the entire earth, touching its core, and, still spreading, to the other side. Eventually, the orb has gone over the entire planet, and, still emanating from your point, and still out through you, it continues out into the galaxy, eating stars and moons, and planets. It dwarfs the sun, then becomes the sun, as the sun is assimilated into all things, through this golden light, and outwards past the galaxy, into further reaches of space, the next galaxy, and the next galaxy, ten galaxies, twenty, a hundred, a thousand, a million, a billion, a trillion. The longer it grows, the shorter the time it has taken to grow seems to you. A second ago, no, less than a second ago, you were watching the sunset. Now you are the universe. And, not only that, but you have changed the universe, the entire universe, and you have changed yourself, as you are that universe, and you are now a golden, glowing light, a light which you met only a second ago, a light which came to you, inside yourself, and started to grow when you embraced it. It is unbelievable to you now that this glorious glowing that was so unfamiliar to you mere seconds before, is now all things; and it is you. But you love it. It is the greatest feeling that you have ever felt. To become this light, and to become all things, something completely and utterly brand new, it has awakened new life across the boundaries of existence, for you, in your life, are reawakened, and, through that, your universe is reawakened, and you are born anew. Suddenly, all life across the universe is vibrating in harmony with yourself, and you feel as if everything makes complete and total sense, and is completely still, working together, for itself. The light now has grown bigger than existence, and existence is a mere speck at the center of this infinite light. At the very center is you, the soul of this light, emanating from your solar plexus, on earth, in this valley, where the sun has set, and the thunder has ceased, and the grass welcomes your body as you lay down, and rest your head, and fall asleep, the light continuing to grow, effortlessly, as you drift off into another place and time, in dreams.

Chapter 16.No Diligence, No Price

In the forest once lived a hamster and a squirrel. The hamster was always very diligent and did all his duties immediately. The squirrel, on the other hand, was very lazy. It would rather enjoy life; without all the annoying tasks that you had to do as a squirrel.

Every autumn, the animals began to gather supplies for hibernation. Squirrels, hamsters, mice and bears retreated to a cozy hideaway in winter to sleep a lot. Only when they got hungry did they wake up to eat. And there had to be something to eat.

So squirrels, hamsters, mice and bears gathered as much food as they could find and hid them in various places. In tree caves, empty bird nests, in the ground or even under stones. They collected more than they needed. Because it could be that other animals found the hidden food and - unknowingly - took the food of another. Or you forgot many hiding places. That could happen - there were many.

So the hamster collected as much as he could. But the squirrel was lazy. He did not feel like collecting every day. It preferred to play by the stream or lay in the grass. When winter came, the squirrel realized that it was quite late and began to gather. Of course, time was not enough and the squirrel was very worried.

It asked the hamster if he would share. The hamster said, "You could have collected enough yourself! Why didn't you do that?

"The squirrel, however, had no excuse and replied," I had so much else to do. That's why I did not make it. Please, dear hamster, you have more than you need. Or should I starve to death? "

"All right," said the hamster, sharing his supplies with the squirrel. The squirrel was happy and thought, "Such a stupid hamster. That was easy. I'll do it again next year! "

When the next autumn came, the hamster again diligently collected food for hibernation. But what was that? The hamster saw the squirrel lying in the grass and dreaming. "What are you doing there? Why don't you collect anything? "Asked the hamster. The squirrel was startled, but again was not excused: "Did you scare me hamster. I'm just taking a break because I've collected so much, "it said.

When the winter came, the squirrel had not collected a nut, not a mushroom, not a cone or seed. With a single nut in his hands, the squirrel went to the hamster and said: "Come on, dear hamster, my whole food was stolen! Only this nut was left to me. What am I doing now? Surely you have more than you need, right? "The hamster shook his head." You have nothing? "He asked. The squirrel replied, "Not a nut, not a mushroom, not a cone or a seed."

The hamster said, "I did not find so much myself this year that it would do for two." The squirrel became angry: "You have not found enough for two? Why didn't you say anything before?

That's pretty mean of you hamster - do you know that? Had I known that, I would have collected myself! "

Then the hamster listened: "You have not collected?" The squirrel swallowed, when it noticed that it had revealed itself: "Well, well. I had a lot to do and then there was little time. "The hamster, however, now realized what he was talking to the squirrel:" That means you lied to me last year. And this year, you just wanted to make it easy for you. I understand that! "Said the hamster angrily.

"But do you really want to starve me?" Asked the squirrel. The hamster shook his head: "No, I will not let you starve to death. I'll give you enough that you do not starve. However, it will be too little to get full. I hope your growling stomach will open your eyes over the winter! "Said the hamster, giving the squirrel a small portion of his supplies.

The squirrel was angry with the hamster and did not seek the blame on himself. It thought, "This mean hamster. Had he told me early enough that he did not have that much, I could have collected something! That's all his fault! "Yes, the squirrel was so upset with himself that it was hard to admit that it had made a mistake.

However, the longer the squirrel was in hibernation and the stomach rumbled, the clearer it became to him that it was all to blame. It had to admit that it had made a mistake. Only then could the squirrel make it better for the next hibernation.

The next autumn, the squirrel gathered day by day. It ran quickly back and forth and collected more of everything. When winter came, the hamster went to apologize. The hamster was very happy about the squirrel's insight!

The squirrel offered the hamster some of his supplies as an excuse. But the hamster had enough supplies this year and said, "I was able to collect enough this year - thank you very much. But other animals may not have been so lucky. They would be very happy if you gave them some of your supplies. "

"That's how we do it!" Said the squirrel and gave some of his supplies to all the animals that did not have that much. The other animals were happy and thanked. But the squirrel said, "I never thought I would say that - but you can actually thank the hamster. He gave me a lesson that I will not forget all my life. "And so the animals thanked the squirrel and the hamster. Since then, all are the biggest friends and help each other - wherever they can!

Chapter 17. Tropical Teasers

Once upon a time, there lived a family of four. There was a mother and a father, who were both very busy with helping people. They loved their work, but oftentimes, it meant that they did not get to spend the time with their children that they wanted. And, there were their twin children. They had a boy and a girl; Alia was the younger twin, but just barely, so the age difference should not count, she always said. And, Arthur was the older twin, and he believed that every second counted, and that meant that he would always be the big bro, and Alia simply had to accept it sooner rather than later! If she could do that, she would have a much easier time dealing with her feelings, after all.

The twins were just like most children their age; they loved to explore the world and play. They loved to spend time with their parents, and they loved to read books all the time. They loved to draw and play games, and they loved to hike and watch movies. But in some ways, they were not like other children their age at all. You see, Alia and Arthur had a very special secret that they did not like to share with anyone. They could speak to animals! No, really; they could speak to animals and have very good, very real conversations with them! They could talk about the weather or about the food that they were eating or about anything else! They could talk about just about anything they wanted to, so long as the animal was willing to do so. And, they were pretty sure that their dad could talk to animals, too, but they were not quite sure.

One day, the whole family had to travel to a tropical island deep in the middle of the ocean. This time, they were on an island that was called Fiji! It was very far in the middle of the ocean, far from just about any other lands. It had beautiful, bright blue water thanks to the fact that it was so far away from everything else, and it had white, sandy beaches that were so big and so soft that they felt like they could live on those beaches and in that sand forever! The twins loved the feeling of the sand under their feet and they felt like it was better than any other sand that they had ever seen before.

Behind them, there were many, many trees growing. The whole land, if you were not looking at the beach, looked like a big blanket of green! It was absolutely gorgeous and as Alia and Arthur walked around on the beach, they felt like they never wanted to leave. "Wow!" said Alia, looking at the beautiful, turquoise water shimmering underneath the sun. There was hardly a wave in sight; it was beautifully calm, and the water was so clear that it was practically transparent!

"You can say that again!" said Arthur as he looked up at a great, big palm tree. Presently, there was a little orange bird sitting in the tree and it was unlike any other bird he had ever seen in his life! It had a strange, green head, but the rest of it was orange. "What a strange looking bird!"

But, the bird looked angry to hear such a thing, and it scoffed and flew away as fast as it could. Arthur felt a little bit sheepish after making the bird angry, but he knew that it would be okay. It would probably just come back later!

Then, he heard another sound—it was a bird that was laughing at them! This bird was bright, lime green and had red little feet and a red throat. "You really messed that one up, kid!" said the bird, laughing and laughing. "Why'd you have to go and make her mad? She's already insufferable enough when she's in a good mood and you must made it worse!

The bird looked like he thought it was the most hilarious thing ever, and yet, Arthur felt bad. "I wasn't trying to make her be in a bad mood!" He crossed his arms and stared at the bird.

"Well, you clearly didn't have to! Don't sweat it too much, kid. She's always offended about something. It is better to simply forget it rather than anything else. Enjoy the sun! You don't look like you're from around here anyway; you may as well enjoy your vacation with all of the other humans! Maybe just toss some French fries my way when you get your food or something!" The bird flapped its wings and flew down closer to stare at Arthur. He didn't seem the least bit surprised that the kid had said a word back to him.

"Wait—you knew I could understand you?" asked Arthur, staring at the bird in shock. He had not expected that at all! He was used to other birds and animals being surprised, so when this one wasn't he was the one feeling all of the surprise instead!

"Yup! I could tell! Do you know how?" asked the bird. He flew down closer to Arthur to look him in the eyes.

Arthur shook his head no, his own eyes growing wider and wider. Was he about to learn some great, new secret that could only be revealed to him in the tropics?

"You have the mark!" the bird said.

"The mark?" asked Arthur, surprised. "What mark?" He wasn't sure that the bird was telling the truth, but he would rather learn that he was fooled than possibly miss out on learning the truth because he was not willing to open up his mind to the possibilities of the world.

"You have a mark on your forehead."

"What mark?" asked Arthur, rubbing at his head. The last time he had checked, there was nothing there at all!

"Yeah! You can see it if you take your fingers and make an L shape and then put it on your head!" The bird bobbed his head up and down convincingly as he stared at Arthur. "When you do that, you know!"

So, Arthur did what the bird told him to, but, when he did, the bird only laughed harder and harder at him! It thought it was the funniest thing in the world! "What's so funny?" asked Arthur, rubbing at his head.

"You put an L on your forehead. Loser! Loser!" squawked the bird louder, practically howling with laughter. But, Arthur didn't think that it was funny at all. He felt sad, in fact; he was very disappointed with how things were going.

"Why are you being so mean?" asked Arthur sadly as he looked down at the beach.

But then, overcame his father. "What's wrong?" asked Arthur's father with a frown on his face.

"Nothing, dad," said Arthur sadly, looking up at the bird one last time.

"Well," said his father, "Can I tell you a cool little secret?"

Arthur perked up. "What is it?"

"You'll have to come with me to see!" So, Arthur and his father went off, away from the obnoxiously loud little bird and went further and further into the center of the island. "I heard that there is a secret place hidden in these woods!" said Arthur's father.

"Oh, what kind of secret place?" asked Arthur.

"You'll have to see it to believe it! But, believe me, it is the greatest place on earth. I've been there before!" So, off they went together, traveling deeper and deeper. The tropical trees and leaves grew thicker and thicker, and they were longer and longer.

There were birds singing everywhere around them. They were beautiful! They sang songs of magic and songs of adventure. They sang songs of kindness and loyalty. They sang songs of all kinds, and Arthur listened very closely to the words as they went. Arthur was quite certain that he could see that his father was listening, too, for his father seemed to turn his head to hear what was going on all around him, just as much as Arthur did. And, that made Arthur smile, for he had had a feeling for a long while that their father could also hear animals the way that he and his sister could. After all, he seemed to know far too much all of the time!

Suddenly, all of the trees disappeared! They were in a clearing, where they could see the great, big tree in the center of the clearing. All above them, they could see the bright, blue sky without a single cloud. It was beautiful! And, underneath the tree, they could see a line up of birds. They were all dancing together! They spun and they swung their wings. They sang and they danced. They jumped and they flipped, and it was the most glorious thing that Arthur had ever seen—and he was seeing it with his father!

But then, something happened. The biggest bird of them all flew down and landed right in front of them. "Ah, Albert!" squawked the bird. "Long time, no see!"

Arthur's father grinned and he held out a hand. "Long time, indeed!" he said to the bird. He looked over at Arthur and winked at him. "You didn't think that you and your sister were the only ones, did you?"

Arthur stared in shock! He had known for a while, but he could not believe it! He was in utter disbelief that his father could also talk to animals! "Does Mom know?" asked Arthur, but his father shook his head. Arthur nodded, looking at the bird thoughtfully. It was probably best that their mother did not know, anyway. She probably would not believe them!

So, from then on, Arthur felt a little bit better about himself. He might have been teased by that bird, but he was not alone! His father could talk to animals just like he and his sister could! His father was just as capable as he was and that was great! So, Arthur smiled at his father and took his hand. "Thanks, Dad," he told him and he felt his father squeeze his hand back.

"I love you, son," said Arthur's father.

"I love you, too!" Arthur replied.

Alia was not the least bit surprised when Arthur told her the truth and all about what they had gone to do that evening. "I told you!!" she cried out. "I! Told! You!" She grinned widely. "Does this mean that we can go on group adventures instead now?"

"You bet it does!" came the sound from behind her, and when Alia turned around, there was their father, waiting for them so they could all go on another hike through the island. "I can't miss out on that great time with you guys, now can I?"

And so, they went on adventures together, and Alia and Arthur felt relieved that it was no longer a secret that they had to keep from everyone else. They were thrilled that they could share with their father, too!

Chapter 18.Where Is Mom Duck?

At a large pond, surrounded by greenery, Mama Duck is just in her nest and is very proud as the offspring hatches from the eggs. The little ducks break the shells and stick their little heads out. Then they wiggle their butts and shake the remaining shell from the bottom.

Mommy Duck affectionately sticks her beak in greeting each one of them. The little ones know immediately that this is the mom. Then Mama jumps into the water and one after the other jumps behind. They swim in a line across the pond - the proud mom in front away.

But, oh dear, what is that? A chick has not hatched yet. It rumbles and rolls in the nest crisscross. With a lot of momentum it falls on the meadow and the egg breaks on a stone. The egg shell flies around and the little duckling shakes a lot. Carefully, it looks around. No, nobody is there. Hm, funny. So the duckling waddles to look for his mom. After a short time the duckling meets a frog. The frog sits on a branch by the water and quacks. "Hurray!" Thinks the duckling. "That must be Mama." It runs to the frog and quacks happily with. The frog looks at the duckling: "What are you doing here?" Asks the frog. The duckling answers: "I quake with you, mamma!" The frog shakes his head: "I'm not your mom!" He says and jumps off. The duckling is sad. Thought it did find his mom. With a hanging head it waddles on. After a few steps, it encounters a bird. The bird chirps happily to himself. The duckling looks at the bird and thinks, "This is not a croak, but it has feathers. Maybe that's my mom. "And then it sits next to the bird and quacks loudly. The bird is outraged: "Why are you covering my beautiful song with your quake?" He asks. Then he picks the duckling upside down and flies away.

Now the duckling is really sad and tears are rolling down his cheeks. "I will never find my mom again!" It quietly sobbing to himself. There comes a fox to the duckling. "Well little duckling, why are you so sad?" Asks the fox. "I am looking for my mom. I'm all alone! "Says the duckling. The fox grins insidiously and says, "Come with me. Together we will find your mom. "

The duckling is happy: "Hurray!" And runs after the fox. After some time, the duckling asks the fox, "How long are we going to walk? We are almost in the forest. "The fox answers:" Do not worry. Your mom is there waiting for you. "

The fox does not have to find the mum. He wants to lure the duckling into the forest to eat it in the shelter of the trees. The fox grins and thinks: "That's too easy. I do not even have to wear the duckling, it goes by itself into the forest. "

Arrived at the edge of the forest, the duckling stops: "It is dark there in the forest!" Says it anxiously. "You do not have to be scared!" Says the fox. "I've hidden your mom there to keep her safe. "Sure, what?" Asks the duckling. The Fox answers in a worried voice, "You know, there are many evil animals that

would love to eat you. But do not be afraid, I'm not one of them!
"

Just as they wanted to move on, a bear stood in the way: "Na fox? Where do you want to go with the duckling? "He asks. The fox ducks in shock: "Hello big bear, where do you come from so suddenly? I only help the duckling to find his mom! "The bear looks at the duckling. Then he asks in a growl voice: "Is that the little duckling?" The duckling jumps up and down: "Yes! The fox hid them in the forest because there are so many evil animals. "

The bear immediately suspects what the fox is up to. "So. So there are many evil animals here. "He growls. Then he looks at the fox suspiciously: "Well, luckily you are not one of them, Fuchs. Right? "The fox shakes his head quickly:" No, no, but of course not. I just wanted to help the poor duckling. "The bear takes the duckling protectively into his paws and says," Well, that's great that the fox has helped you so far. Now I'll do better. Your mom is not in the woods any more. I think she went to the pond to look for you. She misses you very much, you know. "Then he looks again at the fox and asks with a threatening look:" Is it true Fox? "The fox nods quickly with his head:" Yes, yes, now that you say it falls give it to me again. She walked to the pond earlier. "Then the fox looks at the duckling:" Your mom is back at the pond. I completely forgot that, yes. "

So the bear takes the duckling. On the way to the pond, the two meet the bird. The duckling trembles. "What do you have?" Asks the bear. The duckling ducks and whispers: "The bird picked me because I thought it was my mom." The bear looks at the bird and grunts: "Look here in your face, the duckling probably speaks the truth. It's also your duty to help, but you did not help the poor duckling! "Then he takes a deep breath:" We'll talk about that when I get back, "he says and carries on the duckling. The bird flutters off quickly. Next, the two meet the frog. The bear looks at the duckling: "Did the frog also do something to you?" The duckling answers: "No, he just jumped away." The bear looks at the frog angrily and growls: "Here I look into your face, the duckling probably the truth speaks. It's also your duty to help, but you did not help the poor duckling! "Then he takes a deep breath:" We'll talk about that when I get back, "he says and carries on the duckling. The frog hops off quickly. When the two arrive at the pond, the duckling is happy, as it sees the mom. It cheers and jumps headlong into the pond: "Thank you bear! Call it to the bear. "And thank you also to the fox of mine." The bear growls loudly backwards: "You're welcome to play little duckling. And do not worry, I'll certainly thank the fox powerfully. "

When the fox hears this, he pricks his ears in alarm. "Oh my, now it's still my collar," he thinks and runs as fast as he can over all the mountains. Since then, the fox has never been seen again. The bear, however, still keeps a watchful eye on the little duckling, so that never again a clever fox comes to stupid thoughts.

Chapter 19. A brilliant friend

It's a beautiful morning on the rider's yard of Mila's parents. Here live Mila, mom, dad and many horses. Mila likes all of them. Even if they are all different. For example, Shooting Star is very meek. At least to Mila. If Dad does not look, she likes to cling to Sternschnuppe's side with her cheek. Karacho, on the other hand, is very boisterous and wild. But Mila is fine too. Every horse is special in its own way.

As long as Mila can think she wants her own horse. But Dad always says it's too early. And so she helps her dad to feed the horses on the ranch and has even already mucked out one or the other stall alone.

Today is Mila's seventh birthday. She is very excited and hopes to finally get her own horse. She gets up early and wakes her parents. "I've become seven!" She calls at the foot of the parent's bed. The arms have ripped her high in the air. Mum and dad just rub their eyes sleepily.

Slowly Papa straightens up: "Oh Sparrow, that's right, it's your birthday. I almost forgot that. "Mila looks at him suspiciously:" Did not you! You just want to kid me! "Mila's father laughs:" You've seen through me again! You are very clever. That's what you have to get from your mother. "He says and gives mom a kiss on the cheek - before he gets up.

"I'm sorry," Mila snorts and sticks out her tongue. "Do that when you're alone." Then she whizzes down the stairs and shouts, "Now come on. Time for my birthday breakfast! "When Mila arrives downstairs, she is amazed. Usually, their gifts are always set up on the kitchen table. But today she is standing in front of an empty table.

"Sorry darling!" Dad says as he comes down the stairs. "You're up so early that we did not have time to have breakfast." Mila is now looking under the kitchen table. "What are you doing honey?" Asks dad. Mila's head flits between the table and the chair: "Well, what? Where are my presents? "

Then she pushes the chair jerkily aside and jumps up. Beaming with joy, she calls out to her dad, "I'm finally going to get a horse right?" That's why there are no presents here. "

The dad turns on the coffee machine and turns to Mila: "Honey, you know ..." Mila interrupts him - she knows this sound: "Yes, yes, it is too early for a horse." The father nods. "Right! It's still too early. Now we have breakfast first and then it goes to school. This afternoon we pick up your horse.

Mila did not really listen to her dad, "Every time you say it's too early. But I take care of the horses and they all love me. I've never ridden before, but I've cleaned out all the stables, all the horses ... "Mila stops and listens:" Did you just say ... "Mila's father nods. "You little chatterbox. Has it reached you now? "He asks. But Mila storms towards him and falls into his arms. Meanwhile,

Mama has come down and hugs both. "Did your dad tell you so?" She says, kissing Mila's head.

At school, Mila can hardly concentrate. Thousands of questions go through her mind. What does your horse look like? How should she get on the horse's back - as small as she is? Mila cannot wait to get home. When the bell sounds at the end of the last hour, she has already packed everything and runs off like an oiled lightning.

When she reaches home, she immediately runs to her father's stable. "I'm there. We can go. "She puffs her out of breath. She has run all the way. "Man Mila," laughs the father. "Get some air. You're pumping like a cockchafer. "Mila has to reach down to her hips and bend her knees to catch her breath - she's out of breath. "That's OK. Get the keys. I'm waiting for the car. "

The dad puts the food bag aside. "We do not need to leave. I had some time this morning, so I've already got your pony. "Mila is suddenly just like one. Her gaze wanders off the stables. There is only one box that has been empty for a long time. Immediately Mila whizzes away again. But the box is still empty. "Where is it?" She calls.

"The pony is on the big pasture." Replies the father. The big willow. This means the large flower meadow above the stream. Mila can barely walk. Nevertheless, she gives everything and sprints off. Her dad is struggling to come after her. On the way to the pasture, she thinks. "Daddy said pony. I'm worried about that. "She thinks and is happy. "I should go up to a pony."

At the top of the pasture, Mila stops dead. There is her pony. At last! It looks like a shrunken Haflinger. It has a white, shaggy mane, a white, shaggy tail and is light brown all over. Only in the face it has a white spot. It's perfect!

Dad comes with a food bag in his hand. "Well, how do you like it?" He asks softly. "It's perfect," she whispers, squeezing him tightly. "The blaze on the face is very sweet." Mila pulls a carrot out of the bag and lures her pony with it. The pony cautiously sniffs it. The nostrils go very far, but it does not eat the carrot. Instead, the pony sniffs at Mila's dad.

Mila is disappointed: "Isn't she hungry?" She asks her father. But at the same moment, the pony grabs the food bag from his father's hand. Then it turns around and wants to go to a pen. Mila laughs out loud.

"Hey you naughty badger!" Calls Mila's dad and quickly reaches for the reins. Mila is excited: "Did you see that? That was pretty smart! "Mila's dad laughs:" Of course I've seen that. "Then he reaches for the food bag and takes it away from the pony again. "But you're right, that was a brilliant move!"

Mila looks at her dad. "I think he did not like it that much." She laughs. "What's the name of my pony?" Mila's daddy brings the food pouch to safety. "Your pony is a he. And his name is Brilliant, "he says.

Mila shines all over her face: "The name fits like a pot on a lid!" "Like the lid on the pot, you mean." Mila's dad corrects. "Yes, that's what I mean!" Replies Mila. "And now? Am I finally learning to ride? Should I ever climb the pony? "

"Not so hasty!" Says Mila's dad. "No one has ridden on Brilliant yet. You're the first. "Mila jumps up and down with joy and claps her hands. She is so happy that she can hardly stand it.

Mila's dad is getting serious now. "Listen to my little one. Riding a horse is something for experienced riders. If Brilliant gets used to you from the beginning, your new friend needs to learn to fully trust you. "

Mila has also calmed down now. "I understand that, Dad." She says. She thinks of the other horses in the barn and how it was when she first had to carry Karacho. She had to be very careful. Karacho is very spirited and he was very restless; until he got used to Mila.

Mila slowly approaches the Brilliant with the carrot. Brilliant tilts a bit unsteadily with his hooves, as if he is considering what he should think of it. But the scent of carrots triumphs. Carefully, he bites off the carrot. While chewing, Mila gently puts her hand on his forehead. Brilliant closes his eyes for a moment. As if he enjoys the touch.

Finally, Mila puts her hand on his neck. "Quiet my friend," she says and feeds him on. "You're doing really well!" Praises Mila's dad softly. After a short time Mila can stroke her pony on the back. And then slip on the other side even under the neck, without brilliant recoiling. As a reward, there is an apple directly from the tree.

As it turns out, Brilliant loves apples. Because when he sees the apple, he immediately begins to scrape excitedly with his hooves and snort. Mila loves apples too. So Mila takes the first bite and Brilliant gets the rest.

While Brilliant is still enjoying chewing, Mila strokes his forehead again and whispers: "We are becoming the best friends. Is it Brilliant? And best friends share everything. "Brilliant lowers his head and Mila gently places her cheek on his forehead. Brilliant steals Mila again and again easily.

Mila's dad can hardly believe it. He wanted to say something when Mila put her cheek on Brilliant's forehead. But then he saw this intimacy between the two and could not imagine that Brilliant Mila would ever do anything.

The sun is already low and Mila's dad calls her that it's already late. Mila takes Brilliant by the reins and leads him from the pasture into the stable. Brilliant Mila trots all the way left behind.

When Brilliant is standing in his box, Daddy Mila strokes her cheek and says, "Now you're going to eat supper and get you ready for bed, okay? The mom is already waiting. And tomorrow we go on. "Mila nods, squeezes her dad and gives Brilliant another kiss on the forehead:" Sleep well my friend. "She whispers and clings to him again.

Then she walks in to Mama and tells her about her great day at supper. Before going to bed, she presses her mom again firmly and thanks for the wonderful birthday. As much as Mila has experienced today, she does not even need a good night.

Chapter 20. Dreaming of Blue

You are lying in your bed, flat on your back, your legs straight out, your arms flat at your sides, your third eye pointed out, up into the sky, your two eyes closed, your mouth still and shut, your nostrils flowing in and out with oxygen. There is nothing but darkness, black, still and solid, with a light, almost imperceptible vibrating blue glowing through it, as if at the edges of reality, eating away. You breathe, without thinking, your core expands in and out, giving breath to your being, and with each breath, your body becomes lighter, and lighter, until it is so light, you begin to lift up from your bed. Through the sheets, through the blankets, up into the room, you are in the middle of the room, hovering, up, and up, through the ceiling, through the roof, into the sky. You are so relaxed; you do not think to care. You are merely experiencing this, this happening. You must be asleep. Your eyes are closed, and your face is pointing up, but you can see everything below and around you. You see the cars in the streets, parked, their owners, their drivers, still and asleep inside their houses. Farther away, lights are on, and there are slight rumbles, white noise in the quiet of the night. The streetlights are on, and they are glowing, and you feel as if their glows might house numerous, intangible souls, disembodied, as you are now. You float up, and up, and with each distance procured, new sights are visible on the periphery. You see the entire skyline, the edges of the city that houses the population of humans, bleeding into the wilderness, over the foothills, into the mountains, where all is dark, pitch dark. The darkness seems like where you will end up, magnetically drawn, as you go upwards, the lights will dim, becoming farther and farther away, and you will be in darkness. Though you could not stop it if you tried, you would not want to, for this darkness, like a moth to a flame, is what you crave the most. In your sleep, you go up, and you have now reached the clouds. The dots comprising the city below you fade out into this overwhelming gray mist, and you know you have transcended one realm into a new one. You will not look back on the city again, not tonight. Up and up, cloud after cloud, sometimes between clouds, and out of them, you see the pitch darkness, accompanied by the far away stars. There is nothing around you, immediately, put deep purple darkness and the black gray clouds. You go through them and do not know where they end or where they began; somewhere above the city, and now somewhere below space. You reach the edge of the bank of clouds, and opened up to you is a dark purple abyss as far as can be perceived, stretched up to a pitch-black infinite array of space and stars. You know there is a very, very long way to go between the clouds you came from and this space, and as you experience transcending through the layers you become deeper and deeper into the trance you were already in. As you are, you are merely an expanding consciousness, devoid of body, totally light, floating up, by the laws of physics, up and up, forever. You are expanding as you leave the atmosphere of the earth, and, with the expansion, you are lighter and lighter. So light, you may not even exist, and may simply be this setting, this environment, experiencing itself from every angle. Who were you again? And where did you come from? You are now in space, going up, up, and up. The moon becomes very large, shining pure white in the black of the sky. It glows, and its glow is a glow that you can feel in your very being, like an incredible high pitch vibrating through every part of you, whatever you are now, up here, floating, freely, nothing. It is a purifying vibration that transmutes you, even more than this journey before, into something brand new, a total rejuvenation, and you have lost even more of yourself as your progress past the moon, into some new, even more gigantic, impenetrable, imperceptible, giant, black, eternal and infinite abyss. Whereas before you had had fixed points you could recognize above you, being the ceiling, the clouds, space, the moon, now there is nothing, nothing but the stars, which are so far away from you they may as well only exist in your imagination. But, still, and effortlessly, you are making your way towards them, ever so slowly. Rising up, and up, and up, and up, and up, and up, and up, this new being, transmuted by the glow of the moon, so light so as to not even exist, transcending all known borders of the human experience, reality on earth, now in oblivion, and floating, up. While your eyes have been closed the whole time, your perception of sight only occurring in some way completely non-physical and devoid of the body, now it is as if your entire being has closed its sight, for there is nothing but blackness. Now even the stars are imperceptible, somehow, for some reason, though you know they are out there, somewhere. There is only blackness, and, as back then, the slowly revealing electrically charged blue coming out from behind the curtain, the undercurrent, eating away at the pitch-blackness, some kind of energy that exists in the space beyond, always there, interconnected, glowing beneath the surface of our reality. The boundaries of existence are dissolved, as you now realize, this blue is all there is, you are floating up now in a sea of soft electricity, a buzzing, a hum, that vibrates your whole being, the molecules vibrating out into it until they are spread so far apart they seem to be scattered evenly across the whole universe. This buzzing, humming blue, scuttling about across eternity like a swarm of insects, has become you, and it is you as you are floating up, past space, and into a deep, dark sleep, dreaming of blue.

Chapter 21. Lake Louise

My mother had often taken me to Lake Louise (Canada) when I was a child. She would pick a day in winter with good snow. I used to stand outside with my arms out in an effort to test if it were Lake Louise's weather or just a flurry. I would watch the white flakes as they floated down around me, covering the blades of grass, mailboxes, and roofs in the neighborhood.

I would run inside and pull at the bottom of my mother's dress, and she would know immediately what I wanted. She would tell me that we would get there all in good time. Sometimes that meant that I was in for a trip, and other times it meant that we could try another day. She would light a fire in the living room and sit me in front of the television with cartoons echoing in the background. Slowly the smell of bacon and eggs would wrap its magical essences around the corners of our house until it was right beneath my nose. This would give birth to a childish excitement within me because we always had a big meal on lake days.

One of the smells that I remember best from my old house is the smell of the coffee that she would brew every morning. It was earthy and cozy, and it seemed to wrap me up as a child. She always told me that I was not allowed to drink it, and for that reason, I assumed that it must have the sweetest and most pleasant taste of any beverage. Boy, was I surprised when I tried that for the first time?

She would turn on old music with words that seem now to pulse in and out of my memory. I can recall the sound of her voice as she sang along and the way that her dress moved around her as she danced. She was magical in my eyes. Sometimes a sound or smell will take me right back to those mornings when I was a child.

Somewhere when I was lost in the haze of those cartoons, she would bounce in and place a warm meal in front of me. I thought nothing of it then, but it's such a stark contrast to adulthood. I return as often as I can to the loving embrace of my mother.

I would savor each bite, because my mother was an amazing cook, even to a picky eater like myself. The eggs were so fluffy that they would almost melt in my mouth, and the bacon always seemed to have the perfect crisp, something I have never been able to achieve. The fireplace always seemed to heat up one side of my face too much. I would spend my time turning away from the flame and then back as I toasted.

My mom would wait patiently as I finished my meal, and then she would race me upstairs to change into my snow coats, scarves, earmuffs, long underwear, and gloves. I loved the way that our shag carpet felt beneath my toes as I would bound around. I loved racing but hated getting ready.

We would finally be ready to take the drive. She and I would engage in a brief snowball fight before we took our trip. She would then plop me down upon the cold leather seats in the car and draw the seatbelt over my shoulder. I remember being able to smell her floral and vanilla perfume, which is a comforting and persistent memory from my childhood.

The lake was stunning in every season, but when the icy breath of old man winter had covered the world, it was a wonderland. There were these massive mountains that served to complete the backdrop of my favorite piece of wilderness. I can't remember then, but now there is this breathtaking resort on the edge of the lake. I have been there once or twice in adulthood, and I have to say that is a lovely experience.

There is such something special about childhood. The snow-covered pine trees and mountain tops made you believe in magic. The warmth of my jacket and my new gloves did little to keep out the chill, but I was in such a jovial place that I just endured the mild discomfort. My mother would take our ice skates from the trunk of the car, and I was reminded of the fun that we would have.

She would guide my small and wobbly body around the lake, which was completely frozen cover. She would smile and wave at the other people that she knew. With my tiny hand in hers, she would lead me all around the lake. I would marvel at our surroundings and imagine that somewhere in the distant mountains, there must be a yeti. The thought would cause me to scoot closer to my lovely mother.

We would laugh and play games. I was pretty sure that I had the best mom in existence. We would dance along the fresh snow and then glide over Lake Louise. These are some of my fondest memories from childhood. I can recall the joyful but sleepy rides back when I would listen to the sounds of the road and then wake up at home in my own bed.

When it snows, I am reminded of the ways that my mother shaped my childhood. Smiled and the smell of her hair and feeling of my hand in hers. All the meals that she prepared and how she managed to get me everything I ever wanted at Christmas, even though we didn't have much money. The games and the soft and giggly way that she would laugh. Winter was not a dead season to me, but a time for making memories. It was a cozy blur of love and acceptance. One day, I want to be half of the woman that my mother was. I want the blissful and blurry memories of my childhood with her, to be something that I can capture and hold forever.

Chapter 22. The Brilliance of Boreas

Once upon a time, a wee funny creature lived in one of the most remote parts of the planet, down at the bottom of a mountain and deep in the depths of a cave. And that is where he stayed for most of the year, with nobody and nothing to bother him. Nobody knew how to find him, really, but everyone knew who he was, for he came out one time of the year to bring his own special deeds to the world. When he wasn't working the weather, he spent most of his time asleep, dreaming of the next season when he would be awakened to work his fierce magic on the land. He dreamt of huge clouds and dark skies, of chilly nights and crisp bright mornings, of icy rain and blankets of snow. He dreamt of small sprites hiding in the crystalline flakes of snow and in the long columns of ice that formed on the rooftops: these sprites were his offspring, released into the world to bring their sparkle to the darkest time of year. He loved storms and scary things, but he also loved to make the world shine for a few moments in time. He would be awakened when all of the other things of the earth went to sleep or into hiding.

Some call him Jack Frost, others call him Old Man Winter, which is funny because Jack Frost is a young, tiny imp, while Old Man Winter is a grey-bearded Old Man, as his name says. He himself answered to the name Boreas, quick as the wind and cold with determination. He wasn't sure what woke him each year, but he just knew that it was the right time when he started to hear the wind swirl outside and the leaves started to fall to the ground. He would start to stir and dream even harder of cold air and ice and snow. Finally, his bright blue eyes would pop open, and he would clap his hands with glee. Wintertime was finally upon us yet again!

Boreas wasn't interested in the bright sun and brilliant flowers of springtime, no; he wasn't interested in the heat and green of summer; he barely noticed the onset of fall, with the last of the harvests and the festivals of spirits. But he knew that his job, which came around every year, was just about to begin. He lit the candles in his cave, and by their dancing blue flames began to plot and plan how this year's winter would go: would it be colder here and there, or over yonder and dale? Would he conjure up lots and lots of snow, or just a slick sleet of ice? How long would the cold winds rage, and would he have the silly groundhog see his shadow for six more weeks of fun? How delightful it was, this planning and plotting, this wishing and waiting. Winter would have its day, as it did each and every year, the wildest and most unpredictable time of the year—at least in Boreas's mind.

Finally, Boreas would go aboveground, when the temperatures were cool enough for it not to burn his bright white skin. His body was not built for even the slightest heat, so he had to wait until the very last leaves had dropped from the trees. This was the time when many people mistakenly believed that winter was already upon them, but no, it was just the last drops of fall opening the gateway to Boreas's annual onslaught.

The first day of winter, he blew and blew and blew, his tiny mouth conjuring up great winds that tumbled down the mountain and into the valley below. These winds picked up speed, faster and faster, dispersing through the whole wide world of winter. He blew and blew and blew until his own white face began to turn blue. The people down in the world started to rub their hands together in the cold wind, to turn up their collars and pull up their hoods. They put on scarves and gloves to keep them warm when they had to go outside. Boreas himself didn't need any protection from the cold: he absolutely reveled in its chilly embrace.

After the winds settled down and the temperatures remained low and everyone was turning up the heat or building fires in the hearth, he decided that it was time for some storms. So, he set up a little cauldron, his special cauldron made of ice crystals and sky metal, and set it over a cold flame—there was no other place on earth where fire burned blue, not red, and was as cold as the coldest winter day. This icy fire helped Boreas brew his special stew in the special cauldron: he added a pinch of ice, a dash of wind, a spoonful of cold, and stirred it around and around until the mixture darkened like the swirling of thunderclouds overhead. But these were not the thunderclouds of spring bringing sheets and rain to water and re-awaken the land. No, these were the dark, rolling thunderclouds of winter, bringing low darkness over everything, even during the day.

The people down below responded by wearing heavier and heavier coats, ducking into the wind and keeping their errands short. Everyone wanted to be indoors near the heat and near the fire. And this is where Boreas felt almost the proudest at his job: while many people complained of the cold and bluster of winter, it in fact brought them together to spend their time indoors, with each other, warm by the fire and the hearth. It reminded people of the glories of family and friends, of big hearty meals cooked and shared together. It coincided with the most wonderful of holidays, celebrated differently around the world, but always celebrated with a spirit of giving and sharing, of loving and giving thanks. In some places, while the wind and cold raged on outside, there were trees with lights or candles galore, and presents were bought and opened. Toasts were exchanged and gratitude lit the air with its unending grace. Boreas delighted in the sound of children laughing and playing together in their seasonal joy. So, while he did bring the discomfort of cold and wind and darkness to the world, it was with purpose, so that everyone could be reminded of what the most important things in life were: togetherness, and joy, and happiness.

But he also had to make sure that the land got to rest; it had to be cold enough so that the frozen ground got a chance to recuperate from all the efforts it had made the year before in growing food and nurturing animals. Winter was the time for the ground to simply sleep, and Boreas had to keep the temperatures low and the winds high for that to happen. He occasionally brought great storms to meet this purpose, storms that ripped through the sky like a cold knife, bringing sheets of ice and cold rain down to the land. These storms, miserable though they could be for a minute, also brought beauty to the land when they passed: Boreas would allow the sun to peek through at the end of the storm to reveal the sparkling wonderland that had been created by the sheets of ice and frozen rain. The icicles that hung from rooftops made ordinary houses look like castles for royalty. And, besides, the children often loved him for it, because sometimes they got a day off from school just to frolic and play.

His most favorite job, and he saved it for special occasions, was to make snow. Great, big, billowing piles of snow. Sometimes, Boreas actually got in trouble because he made too much snow for one area or the other. You know, those times when two or three feet of snow are dumped all at once in a place; that's when Boreas is especially happy or a little bit hyper. But, oh how he loved to make snow! He loved to watch the thick thatch of snow drifting down gently from the sky. Or the hard pellets of snow that accumulate on the ground like sand until there's enough of it to make a pile. He loved the way the heavy blanket of snow covered the landscape, wiped it clean of all detail. He thought that the world looked new and innocent after a big snowfall. He used all of his best tools for the snow, the cauldron over the blue fire, his magic breath, his little crystalline wand that looked like the finest icicle ever. He conjured up the snow, again, for the sheer delight of it, to watch the people react, to protect the ground and to prepare it for spring.

It was harder than it used to be, alas, to conjure the snow. The warm winds from the south, from the warming air fought him on it from time to time. The ground stayed warmer for longer with each passing year, making it harder to lay down that beautiful white blanket. It saddened him to think of his great icebergs breaking down into the water, the melting of ancient ice that he had so long ago created, but he wouldn't let it stop him entirely. He kept making snow, even if it was a little bit less each year. He couldn't resist watching the adults behave like children, out there in the snow, making snowballs and creating figures out of snow. He couldn't resist listening to the children play and run their sleds down the hillsides. He especially loved it when the kids would come up with some new idea for the snowman: snow cats and dogs, snow frogs on occasion, snow castles like they'd seen in the movies. It was pure creativity at its very best, just using all that lovely white snow as a blank canvas for the imagination. In some places, Boreas made it possible for the people to make an entire village out of snow figures, with kings and queens and knights and princesses. It was such a lovely sight to see!

One of the best things about winter to Boreas—besides all of the holiday celebrations and besides the beautiful blankets of snow—

was how quiet it could be. Boreas treasured that peacefulness, that quiet that came over the land when everything was resting, the ground was sleeping and the animals were hibernating. Winter was a time of hush, while the birds were in the south and the trees were sleeping, the animals were huddled in their burrows with their gathered stocks of food. Everything would awake with the coming of spring, but for now, the land was still and quiet, just anticipating. This kind of quiet should be treasured, as it only comes once a year. And when it all lay under a thick blanket of snow, it was as if the land were like a person, snuggled in a very soft bed under a very soft blanket, with only a sliver of pale moonlight to break the darkness. It was quiet and cold, while everyone inside was warm and comfy, all tucked into their beds, letting winter do what winter does and dreaming of the next big snowfall.

Conclusion

You deserve to live the best life that you can, and that is a life that is free from stress, free from pain, free from the distractions of reality, and safe. You deserve to live a life in which you are more than capable of controlling your own reactions to the world. Remember, there is a vast difference between being able to control the world around you and being able to control the reactions that you have. Remember that, at the end of the day, you can control your behaviors. You can control your thoughts. Between controlling the thoughts and feelings that you have, you can choose to remove the power that stress has over your life. Your life filled with stress is a choice that you choose to live. You can choose to let go of the stressors that you have. You can choose to step back, declare that you are done with the stress that surrounds you, and distance yourself from it all. You can make that decision for yourself without much of a problem or a hassle at all; all you have to do is declare it so.

As this book wraps up to a close, remember to maintain these principles throughout your life. Do not forget the power of a simple breath; do not forget that, at the end of the day, your breath that you take can control the filter through which you see the world around you. It can change the way that you see the very world as it unveils itself to you. That breath can be the difference between living a life filled with stress and uncertainty and discovering one that you can take control.

Do not forget the power of mindfulness and of meditation. If your stress ever appears to be too much for you, you have options that you can take. You have ways that you chose to control the way that you feel. You can learn to counter and combat that stress to allow yourself to escape relatively unscathed from its grasp.

Do not forget to recognize that your stress will always compound on itself. Do not forget that stress has its own tendency to constantly push itself, spiraling out of control. Remember that you have the power to stop it in its tracks; you have the power that you can use to control the way that you feel to prevent that stress from becoming something impossible that you cannot control. You have the power that you can use to prevent yourself from struggling more than you have to.

And at this point, you may be wondering, "Well, what now?" And the answer is simple. Now, it is time to put everything to work. Now it is time to test the theories that you have been given. It is time to take those techniques that you have been provided and push them onto yourself. It is time to figure out precisely how you can better yourself and then begin to see how they work for you. It is time to begin figuring out the ways that you can control yourself; that you can take back that quiet control of yourself and live your life the way that you want. It is time to fight back, to release that stress and return back to your own quiet life that you can live your way, with more control than you have ever had access to before.

Lightning Source UK Ltd.
Milton Keynes UK
UKHW021515101120
373146UK00003B/278